Page
92

HOLT SOCIAL STUDIES
COMMUNITIES

JoAnn Cangemi
General Editor

HOLT, RINEHART AND WINSTON, PUBLISHERS
New York ● Toronto ● Mexico City ● London ● Sydney ● Tokyo

General Editor
JoAnn Cangemi

is Professor of Education and Director of Graduate Studies in Education at Nicholls
State University, Thibodaux, Louisiana. She received her Ph.D. in elementary education
from Louisiana State University. Prior to her university work, Dr. Cangemi taught in the
public elementary schools for ten years. She has served as a consultant in social
studies curriculum development to numerous public and private school systems. She is
the author of a number of articles in professional journals. For ten summers she taught
in Europe as part of a foreign exchange program. She was a 1981 recipient of the Merit
Teacher Awards given by the National Council for Geographic Education.

Contributing Writers
Pat Cuthbertson

is a writer who lives in Santa Cruz, California. She received a B.A. in English literature
from the University of California at Santa Cruz, graduating with General College Honors.
She has written material for Language Arts and Social Studies texts. She has two sons
in whose classes she has worked as a volunteer for several years.

Tom Cuthbertson

is a writer of "how to" books who lives in Santa Cruz, California. He received a B.A. in
literature from the University of California at Santa Cruz and an M.A. in writing from
San Francisco State. He has written a number of technical manuals, as well as material
for Language Arts and Social Studies texts. He has done volunteer work in his sons'
elementary classrooms.

James A. Harris

is an elementary principal in the D.C. Everest Area School District, Schofield,
Wisconsin. He graduated from Miami University, Oxford, Ohio, and received his
Master's degree in Curriculum and Instruction from the University of Wisconsin. Mr.
Harris began his teaching career while a VISTA volunteer and later served in the
Wisconsin Native American Teacher Corps. For ten years he taught kindergarten and
primary grades in Wisconsin schools. Mr. Harris is a frequent consultant to school
systems and educational corporations. He has published many articles in professional
magazines and journals.

James J. Rawls

is a native of Washington, D.C. He received a B.A. from Stanford University and a Ph.D.
from the University of California, Berkeley. Since 1975, Rawls has been a history
instructor at Diablo Valley College. His articles and reviews have appeared in such
publications as *The Journal of American History, The Wilson Quarterly, The American
West,* and *California History.* He is the author of *Indians of California: The Changing
Image,* and coauthor of *California: An Interpretative History* and *Land of Liberty.* Rawls
has served as an historical consultant on numerous films and on a series of television
programs funded by the National Endowment for the Humanities.

"A Day in the City," ©Marie Keegan/Jay Johnson Gallery

Photo and art credits begin on page 255.

Copyright © 1986, 1983 by Holt, Rinehart and Winston, Publishers
All Rights Reserved
Printed in the United States of America
ISBN: 0-03-001784-X
5678 039 987654321

TABLE OF CONTENTS

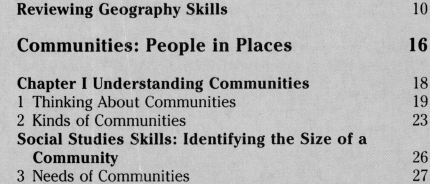

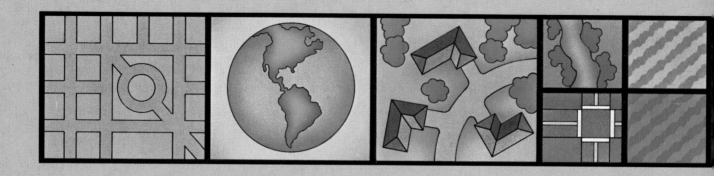

MAPS AND GLOBES

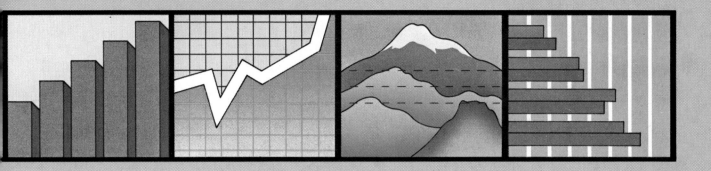

CHARTS, GRAPHS, AND DIAGRAMS

reviewing
GEOGRAPHY skills

Suppose someone asked how to find your house. How would you explain it? You might draw a **map.** A map is a picture of a place. A map can show the whole earth or just a part of it. Maps show where things are and how far they are from each other. People use maps to find out how to get from one place to another.

People also use maps to find out what the world is like. Maps show land and water. They can also show things that people build on the earth, such as roads, bridges, buildings, and towns. In this book, there are many different kinds of maps to help you learn about the earth.

Symbols and Map Keys

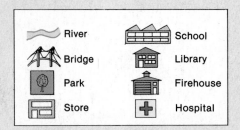

On a map, small drawings called **symbols** are used to show real things. A map symbol stands for something real. Often it is drawn to look like the thing it stands for.

On this page are some symbols you might find on a map. Try to guess what each one stands for. A symbol like this one ⚡ is easy to guess. You may have guessed that it is the symbol for a bridge. A symbol like this ⊞ is harder to guess.

How can you figure out the meaning of a symbol you cannot guess? Most maps have a

map key to help you. The map key tells you the meaning of each symbol.

The map on this page is a **street map.** It shows the names and locations of streets in a neighborhood. It also shows the locations of important places. Find the map key on the street map. Now you can see that this symbol ⊞ stands for a hospital. This symbol 🔲 stands for a store. How many stores would you pass if you took a walk on Hope Street? Now find the symbols for a firehouse, a library, and a school. Then find each building on the map.

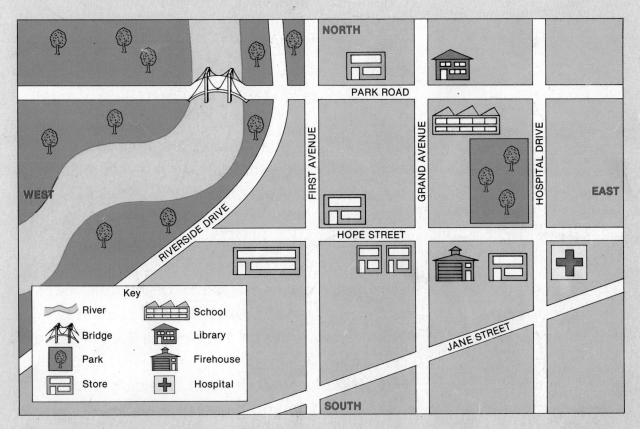

Finding Directions

A map shows directions—north, south, east, and west. The map on page 11 uses words to show each direction. Other maps show only north. How do you know the other directions? South is always opposite north. When you face north, east is to the right. West is to the left.

Some maps use a drawing called a **compass rose** to show directions. The **N** pointer on the compass rose shows the direction of north. What do the **S, E,** and **W** pointers show?

Finding Distance

A map can also be used to measure distance. To find out how far away a place is, you could look at the **distance scale.** A distance scale is a measuring line on a map that can be used to tell how far one place is from another.

Here are two distance scales. One measures kilometers and one measures miles. The top scale says that 2 centimeters on the map stand for 10 kilometers on the earth. This means that one centimeter stands for 5 kilometers. The bottom scale says that one inch on the map equals 8 miles on the earth.

Look at the map on page 13. How can you find out how many kilometers the edge of Brookline is from downtown Boston? First, use a ruler to measure the distance on the map. This distance is 2 centimeters. Then measure 2 centimeters on the scale. Each centimeter on the scale equals 2 kilometers, so 2 centimeters equal 4 kilometers. It is 4 kilometers from the edge of Brookline to downtown Boston.

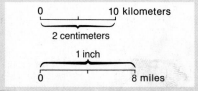

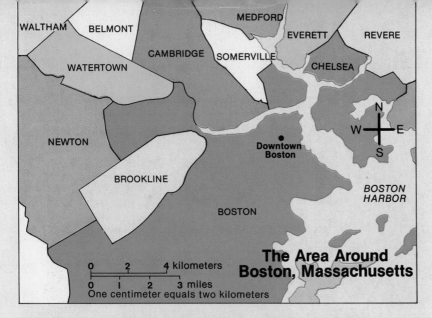

The Area Around
Boston, Massachusetts

0   2   4 kilometers
0 1 2 3 miles
One centimeter equals two kilometers

Using a Map of Our Country

A map like the one on this page shows only a small part of the earth. This map shows only the area around a big city, Boston. The map on pages 14–15 shows a much larger place. This map is a picture of your country, the United States of America.

Notice that the map of the United States is divided into 50 parts. Each part shows the shape of one of the 50 states. Find your state on the map. Use your finger to trace the shape of your state. How many other states touch your state? Name them.

Using a Globe

A **globe** can show all of the earth. A globe is a round model of the earth. It shows the shapes of all the earth's land and water.

You can see the shape of your country on the globe on this page. What else can you see?

In this book, you will use many kinds of maps and globes. Some you already know about. Some will be new to you. All the maps and globes can help you learn more about the earth you live on.

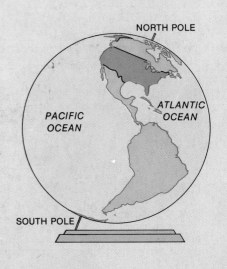

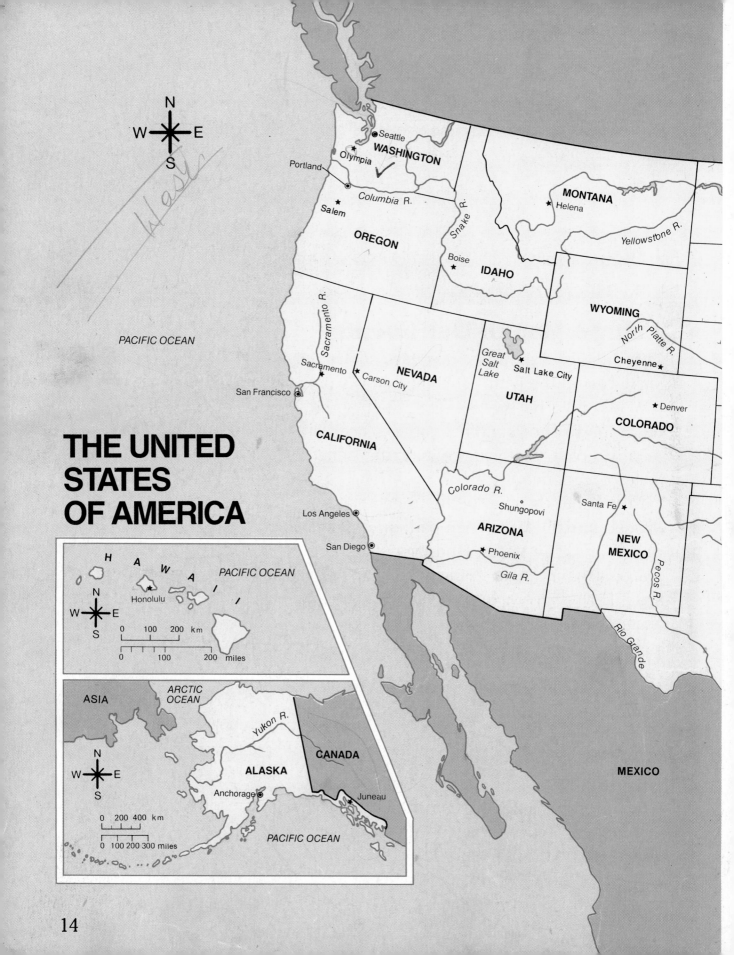

THE UNITED
STATES
OF AMERICA

PACIFIC OCEAN

N
W — E
S

Seattle
★ WASHINGTON
Olympia
Portland
Columbia R.
Salem
OREGON
Snake R.
MONTANA
★ Helena
Yellowstone R.
Boise
IDAHO
WYOMING
North Platte R.
Cheyenne ★
Sacramento R.
Great Salt Lake
Salt Lake City
NEVADA
Sacramento ★ Carson City
UTAH
COLORADO
★ Denver
San Francisco
CALIFORNIA
Colorado R.
Shungopovi
Santa Fe ★
Los Angeles
ARIZONA
NEW MEXICO
Pecos R.
San Diego
★ Phoenix
Gila R.
Rio Grande
MEXICO

H A W A I I
Honolulu ★
PACIFIC OCEAN
N
W — E
S
0   100   200 km
0   100   200 miles

ASIA
ARCTIC OCEAN
Yukon R.
CANADA
ALASKA
N
W — E
S
Anchorage
Juneau
0 200 400 km
0 100 200 300 miles
PACIFIC OCEAN

14

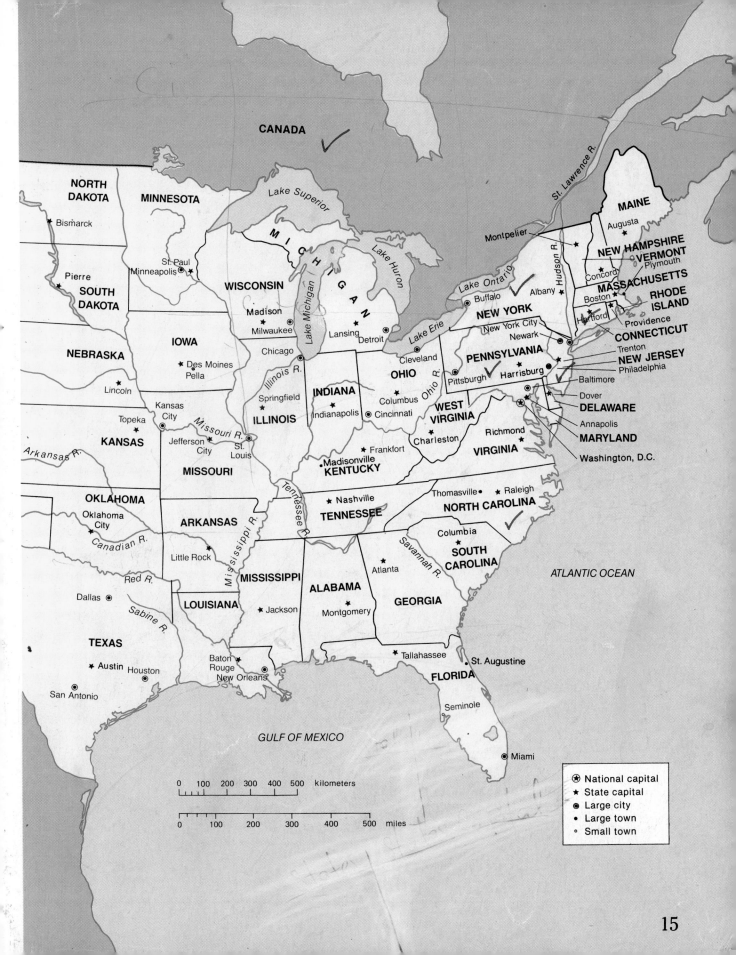

CANADA

NORTH DAKOTA

MINNESOTA

Lake Superior

MICHIGAN

MAINE

Augusta

St. Lawrence R.

• Bismarck

St. Paul

Minneapolis

SOUTH DAKOTA

WISCONSIN

Lake Michigan

Lake Huron

Montpelier

Hudson R.

NEW HAMPSHIRE

VERMONT

Plymouth

Concord

MASSACHUSETTS

RHODE ISLAND

Pierre

Madison

Milwaukee

Lansing

Detroit

Lake Ontario

Buffalo

Albany

Boston

NEBRASKA

IOWA

Des Moines

Pella

Chicago

Illinois R.

Cleveland

Lake Erie

NEW YORK

New York City

Newark

Hartford

Providence

CONNECTICUT

Lincoln

Springfield

INDIANA

OHIO

Columbus

Ohio R.

PENNSYLVANIA

Pittsburgh

Harrisburg

Trenton

NEW JERSEY

Philadelphia

Kansas City

Topeka

Jefferson City

St. Louis

Indianapolis

Cincinnati

WEST VIRGINIA

Charleston

Baltimore

Dover

DELAWARE

Annapolis

MARYLAND

Washington, D.C.

KANSAS

Arkansas R.

MISSOURI

Madisonville

KENTUCKY

Frankfort

Richmond

VIRGINIA

OKLAHOMA

ARKANSAS

Tennessee R.

Nashville

TENNESSEE

Thomasville

Raleigh

NORTH CAROLINA

Oklahoma City

Canadian R.

Little Rock

Mississippi R.

Columbia

SOUTH CAROLINA

Red R.

MISSISSIPPI

ALABAMA

Atlanta

Savannah R.

ATLANTIC OCEAN

Dallas

Sabine R.

LOUISIANA

Jackson

Montgomery

GEORGIA

TEXAS

Austin

Houston

Baton Rouge

New Orleans

Tallahassee

St. Augustine

San Antonio

FLORIDA

Seminole

GULF OF MEXICO

Miami

0 100 200 300 400 500 kilometers

0 100 200 300 400 500 miles

⊛ National capital
★ State capital
⊙ Large city
• Large town
○ Small town

15

UNIT
1

Communities:
People in Places

Here comes the parade! The band leads the way. The parade is part of a festival held in this town each year. The parade is something people in this community enjoy together.

Most people live together in communities. In this unit, you will learn about different kinds of communities. You will find out how people live in them. You will read about the many things people in communities do together.

CHAPTER 1
Understanding Communities

Almost everyone lives in a community. There are many kinds of communities all over the world. Some communities are big cities. Some are small towns. The picture on this page shows a small town. Is your community big or small?

At the end of this chapter, you should be able to:

○ Explain what a community is.
○ Name three kinds of communities.
● Read symbols for communities on a map.
○ Name some of the important needs of communities.
● Use a compass rose.

1 Thinking About Communities

A **community** is a place and the people who live there. Most communities begin and grow in places where people often meet. For example, people may come together to live where main roads meet. They may start a community at such a meeting place. People may use a river for travel and begin a community along its banks. Many communities have grown along the ocean at places where ships land.

People all over the world live in communities. Some communities look very much like yours. Other communities look very different. The pictures on this page show communities in different parts of our country.

community
a place and the people who live there

People in communities do things together. Sometimes they work together. Sometimes they learn together. Many times they get together to have fun. Many people working together can often do more than one person or family working alone. The pictures on this page show some of the ways people in communities do things together. What are some activities people in your community do together?

In some ways, most communities are alike. They usually have homes, schools, hospitals, stores, and businesses. People of all ages live there. People do many kinds of jobs.

In most communities, people with the same interests form groups. A group may get together to clean up their community or to form a community band or chorus. Some groups of people follow the same **customs**. A custom is a special way a group of people does things. It may be one group's custom to honor their community's past each year. They may have a parade or a special festival. Sometimes small groups of people do things together. At other times, the whole community does things together.

custom
the special way a group of people does something

senior citizen
an older person who has stopped working at a job

retire
to stop working at a job after reaching a certain age

Communities are sometimes different from each other. Look at the pictures on this page. One shows people from a community in which customs are shared. The other shows people in a community for **senior citizens.** Many of these older people have **retired,** or stopped working at jobs, after reaching a certain age. A senior-citizen community has homes and stores. But a senior-citizen community may need tennis courts more than a playground. Why do you think this is so?

Amish buggy parking lot, Sugarcreek, Ohio

Senior citizens, Sunrise Lakes, Florida

Section Review

Write your answers on a sheet of paper.
1. What is a community?
2. Name two ways communities can be different.
3. Name two ways communities can be alike.
4. What groups do you belong to in your community?

2 Kinds of Communities

Let's look at three kinds of communities. The first is called a **city.** A city is a large center where many people live and work. The city in the picture is Houston. It is in the state of Texas.

People in a city often live close together. Some people live in apartment buildings. Others live in houses. If you live in a city, you do not know everyone in your community. About 1¼ million people live in Houston. That is more people than any one person could know!

Like many cities, Houston has its own airport. It also has a sheltered place where ships land, called a **harbor.**

Houston has many big office buildings. It has schools, hospitals, theaters, and museums. Houston also has a big sports stadium called the Astrodome.

Like other cities, Houston is a very busy place.

city
a large center where many people live and work

harbor
sheltered place where ships land

Main Street in a suburb

Where people live in a suburb

suburbs
smaller communities
that surround a city

Most large cities are surrounded by smaller communities, called **suburbs.** About one out of every three Americans lives in a suburb.

One suburb is River Forest, Illinois. About 13,000 people live in River Forest. Like most suburbs, River Forest is a community of houses and stores. It also has schools, hospitals, and libraries.

Many people who live in suburbs travel to nearby cities to work or shop for special things. Many people in River Forest go to the nearby city of Chicago. Do you live in a suburb? If you do, what big city is near you?

A third kind of community is a small **town**. A town is a community that is smaller than a city. One small town is Freedom, Maine. About 450 people live in Freedom.

People who live in small communities usually know each other. Some people may live on farms far apart. But many of the people in the community come together often. These people may shop in the same stores, use the same bank, or attend the same school.

town
a community that is smaller than a city

Section Review

Write your answers on a sheet of paper.
1. Name three kinds of communities.
2. Name two ways in which the largest kind of community differs from the smallest kind.
3. Name the kind of community you live in.

Identifying the Size of a Community

Communities can be many different sizes. Some, such as Chicago, Illinois, are very large. Other communities, such as Chapin, Illinois, are very small. How can you tell how big a community is? Sometimes, if you study a map key, the symbols will tell you.

A circle, or dot ●, is often the symbol for a community. A large, dark dot may show a large community. What kind of dot may show a small community?

A star ☆ may be used to show the **state capital.** This is the city where the rules for the state are made. Look at the map of Illinois on this page. What is the state capital?

state capital
the city where rules for the state are made

═══ Practice Your Skills ═══

1. Is Cedarville or Rockford larger?
2. Name the smallest communities shown.
3. What city is closest to the state capital?

3 Needs of Communities

Communities need many things. Some of these things are called **natural resources.** A resource is something we need and use. A natural resource is something we use from nature, such as air, soil, plants and animals, trees, and water. The pictures on this page show some ways a community may use water. In what other ways might a community use water?

Communities also need **energy,** or power to make things work. Energy is needed to supply heat and electricity for the homes, factories, and other buildings in a community. Natural resources can be used to make energy. Coal, for example, is a natural resource. Some communities burn coal to make energy.

natural resources
things we use from nature, such as water, air, soil, plants, and animals

energy
power to make things work

human resources
people whose work and skill are used by a community

Communities need another important resource—people. People are a source of work and skill for a community. They are called the **human resources** of a community.

A community uses its human resources in many ways. Some people are skilled in building roads. Others work to keep the roads in good repair. Some people put up buildings. Other people may paint the buildings or keep them safe from fire.

Look at the pictures on this page. How are human resources being used? What other jobs do people in communities do?

When people live together in a community, they need some way of making sure things get done. Schools must open in the fall. Snow must be removed from streets after a storm.

How can the people of a community keep track of all these things? The community forms a **government.** A government is the group of people who manage a community, and their way of managing. Every community needs some kind of government.

One thing a government does is make rules for the people in a community. These rules are called **laws.** Laws are written to make the community a safe and peaceful place for everyone. Traffic laws, for example, are rules about how to use the community's streets. Without such laws, people could drive down highways backwards or park in the middle of the street! What traffic law is shown in the picture on this page?

government
the group of people who manage a community, and their way of managing

laws
rules that a government makes for the people in a community

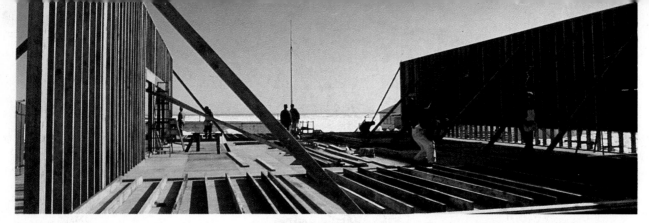

Building a new school in Alaska

Another job of the community government is keeping track of the community's money. The needs of a community have to be paid for. People pay for these community needs in a special way. People must give part of the money they earn to the community. The money given up is called a **tax.** The community government uses the taxes to pay for what the community needs. Taxes pay for schools, libraries, police forces, and many other community needs.

A community is people. People in communities share interests, needs, natural resources, and government.

tax

money that people must give to a government to pay for community needs

Section Review

Write your answers on a sheet of paper.
1. Name three natural resources a community needs.
2. Why does a community need energy?
3. How does a community pay for things it needs?
4. Name three ways human resources are used in your community.

JANE ADDAMS

Jane Addams was born in Cedarville, Illinois, in 1860. When she was six, her father took her to a city. They traveled through many neighborhoods. Some were run-down and crowded. Jane saw children in ragged clothes. She saw people who were poor. Many looked sick or hungry.

Jane Addams never forgot these poor people. Years later, in 1889, she opened Hull House in a poor Chicago neighborhood. Hull House was a place where people could go for help. There they found help in many ways.

At Hull House, people from other countries were taught English. Parents could leave their children to be cared for while they worked. The children played, sang, and listened to stories.

Jane Addams helped other poor children too. In those days, many young children worked long hours in crowded rooms called sweatshops. In summer sweatshops were very hot. In winter they were very cold. The children ran dangerous machines.

Jane Addams fought to change laws about children working. In 1893, a new law was passed. This law helped protect children from bad working conditions.

Jane Addams worked to help poor people all her life. In 1931, she won the Nobel Peace Prize. This is a special prize given to people whose work has helped others.

Finding Directions on a Map

How do you find directions on a map? On a simple map, the four main directions might be written on the top, bottom, and sides like this.

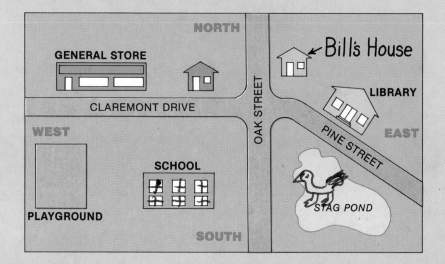

On other maps, an arrow like this ᴺ↑ might be used. **N** is a short way of writing north. The arrow points in the direction of north.

On some maps, directions are shown on a compass rose. The long points on the rose show you where to find the four directions. You know that **N** stands for north. What do **S, E,** and **W** stand for?

Did you notice the four short lines on the compass rose? These lines stand for the in-between directions. The in-between directions are those that are halfway between the main directions.

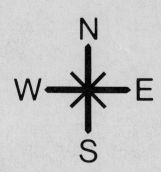

Look at the map of Freedom, Maine, on this page. In what direction is Sandy Pond? Sandy Pond is really halfway between south and east. A shorter way of saying this in-between direction is southeast.

The compass rose at the right shows the four in-between directions. What are they?

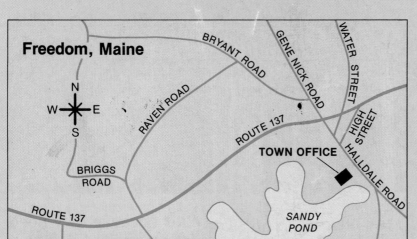

Practice Your Skills

1. What direction lies between south and west?
2. What two words are used to begin the in-between directions? What words are used to end them?
3. Look at the map of Bill's neighborhood on page 30. In what part of the neighborhood is the library? Where is the playground?

2 A Community Is People

People live in communities because they need each other. Most people do not take care of all their own needs. They depend on what other people do. People in communities do jobs that help meet the needs and wants of everyone in the community.

At the end of this chapter, you should be able to:
- ○ Explain the terms "goods" and "services."
- ○ Explain how people supply goods and services for a community.
- ○ List some of the duties people have in their community.
- ● Read a bar graph.

1 Working in a Community

When people work at jobs, they earn money. The money they earn is called **income.** With their income, people buy things they need or want.

Some people help their community by working to produce things other people need, such as shoes or chairs. These things are called **goods.** What are some of the goods that you use?

income

money a person earns

goods

things people make, such as shoes or chairs

Cutting cloth in a clothing factory

Baking bread

People pay for goods with some of their income. Look at the chart below. This farmer has earned income by growing and selling corn. Then he spends some of his income. He buys goods such as a tractor or a truck.

The factory worker earned income by making tractors. This worker may use some of her income to buy corn and many other goods.

In communities, people can usually get the goods they need. A community usually has stores where people can buy all kinds of goods. A large community usually has more stores and more kinds of goods to buy than a small community. What kinds of goods can you buy in your community?

People may also use some of their income to pay for **services.** These are useful acts that people do for others, often for money. A person pays a taxi driver for a ride in a taxi. A store pays a store clerk to sell its goods. Look at the pictures on this page. What other services do they show? Tell how these services help people.

Most people cannot perform all the services they need. They depend on the many services that other people supply. They also depend on the services that the community supplies, such as garbage pickup or street repair.

In communities, people can usually get the services they need. The larger the community, the more services it offers. Large cities, for example, usually have many museums, parks, libraries, and restaurants.

services
useful acts that people do for others, often for money

consumer
a person who buys and uses goods or services

producer
a person who makes goods or performs services

volunteer
a person who works without pay

When people buy and use goods or services, they are called **consumers.** When people make goods or perform services, they are called **producers.** Most people are both consumers and producers. A farmer is a producer when growing and selling corn. A farmer is a consumer when using some income to buy a tractor. Both consumers and producers are important to a community.

Some people do work in the community without being paid. These people are called **volunteers.** Many volunteers give up their free time to do things for the community. The picture shows people working without pay to help a community. What other kinds of work do volunteers do?

In a community, all kinds of human resources are needed. People depend on each other in many ways.

Community flower-planting project

Section Review

Write your answers on a sheet of paper.
1. List three examples each of goods and services.
2. Name two ways a volunteer can help a community.
3. Tell how a carpenter can be both a consumer and a producer.

2 Running a Community

All communities have **leaders.** These women and men have two main jobs, or duties. They make plans for a community. They also help show the community the best way to carry out these plans. These leaders make many choices for the community. They may decide to plant more trees in a park or build a new school. They may decide to put up a new stop sign or clean the streets more often. Community leaders also make choices about how much money can be spent to do these things.

Who chooses community leaders? The men and women who are members of a community, or its **citizens,** choose their leaders. They do this by voting. In both large and small communities, citizens vote for, or **elect,** their leaders. Who are some of the leaders in your community?

leader
a person who makes plans and helps show a community the best way to carry out these plans

citizen
a person who is a member of a community

elect
to choose by voting

Candidate speaking at a county fair

Some leaders make the laws. They help plan what laws are needed to solve community problems. Sometimes they pass new laws, and sometimes they change old laws.

mayor
the head of a
community government

The **mayor** is usually the head of a community's government. The mayor helps to make sure that the laws of the community are obeyed. The mayor also works to see that the community has all the services it needs.

appoint
to choose

The mayor chooses, or **appoints,** other women and men to help run the community. The chart on this page shows some of the leaders the mayor might appoint. The mayor must make good choices for the community government to work well.

The leaders of a community work together. They listen to what the citizens say. Leaders and citizens try to make their community a good place to live and work.

Community Leaders	Symbols
Police Chief	
Fire Chief	
Librarian	
Head of Planning Board	
Health Officer	
Sanitation Chief	

All of the citizens in a community have **responsibilities,** or duties. It is their job to obey the laws. Citizens are responsible for paying taxes. It is also their job to elect community leaders. The picture on this page shows another responsibility of a good citizen. Have you ever helped clean up your community?

responsibility
duty

Section Review

Write your answers on a sheet of paper.
1. How do citizens choose community leaders?
2. List three of a citizen's responsibilities.
3. What are some of the things that you are responsible for in your classroom?

Reading a Bar Graph

Ms. Ray owns a lawn and garden shop. She sells many goods, including lawn mowers.

Suppose Ms. Ray wants to show in a clear, simple way how many mowers she sold each day of the week. She could make a **bar graph** like this.

bar graph
a picture using bars of different lengths to show information

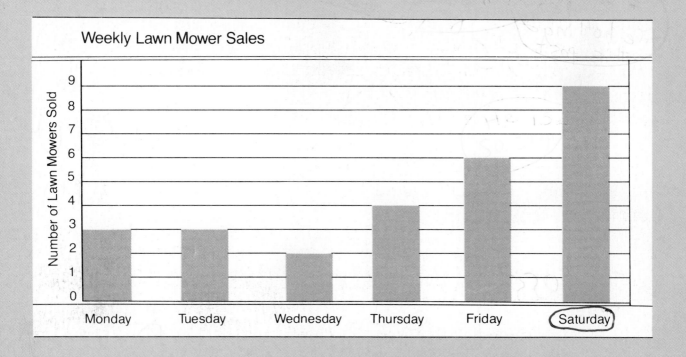

The days of the week are shown at the bottom of the graph. Along the left side of the graph are the numbers 0 to 9. These stand for the number of lawn mowers sold. The bars show how many lawn mowers were sold on each day. The taller the bar is, the more mowers were sold.

42

To find out how many lawn mowers were sold on Thursday, do this.

1. Put your finger on the bottom of Thursday's bar. Then move your finger up to the top of the bar.
2. Look at the numbers at the left side of the graph. At what number does the bar stop? You are correct if you said four. Ms. Ray sold four mowers on Thursday.

How can you figure out on which day the most mowers were sold? Just look for the tallest bar. Then find the day underneath the bar.

How can you figure out on which day the smallest number of mowers was sold? Look for the shortest bar.

━━ Practice Your Skills ━━

1. On which two days was the same number of mowers sold?
2. How many mowers were sold on Thursday? on Friday?
3. Why do you think there are no sales shown for Sunday?

Harvest Festivals Farming is a very important job in our country. It is also a very difficult job. Farmers work hard planting crops and taking care of them. They are glad when their crops have grown well. They know they will be able to earn extra money from their crops if they have plenty to sell.

Harvest time comes when crops are fully grown and ready to be picked and taken to market. After the work of the harvest is over, it is time for farmers to relax. Sometimes people in a farming community have a harvest festival to celebrate the good crop.

Many kinds of harvest festivals are held in the United States today. A forest festival is held in West Virginia. People there celebrate the good crop of trees that has grown. In Massachusetts, people have an apple festival. In Ohio, people take part in a pumpkin festival.

Apple festival, Harvard, Massachusetts

44

America

Pumpkin festival, Circleville, Ohio

Cherry festival parade, Traverse City, Michigan

One of the largest harvest festivals in the United States is the National Cherry Festival in Traverse City, Michigan. Each summer, after the cherry crop is harvested, the festival begins. Large tents are put up in town. People eat cherry pancakes and drink cherry juice. Cherry ice cream is made, and people go to cherry ice cream parties. Hundreds of people come to visit the cherry orchards. Even the name of the main street is changed for just one week out of the year. It is called Cherry Lane, of course!

During the week of the National Cherry Festival, dances, parades, and contests are held. People of all ages join in the fun.

Harvest festivals all over the country are a joyful time. They are the farmers' way of sharing the crops they grow. They are also the farmers' way of rewarding themselves for a job well done.

UNIT REVIEW

Word Work

Write the sentences below on a sheet of paper. Fill in the blanks with the correct words from the list.

suburbs   custom   consumer   elect

1. A ____ is the special way a group of people does something.
2. ____ are communities that surround a city.
3. A ____ is a person who buys goods and services.
4. People vote to ____ their community leaders.

Knowing the Facts

Write your answers on a sheet of paper.
1. What is a community?
2. Why do people live in communities?
3. Name some of the needs of communities.

Using What You Know

Choose one of the following activities to do. Follow the instructions given here.
1. Make two lists—one of goods, the other of services—that are supplied in your community.
2. Make a bar graph to show how many glasses of milk or juice you drink in a week.

Skills Practice

Use the following map and map key to answer the questions below. Write your answers on a sheet of paper.

1. What is the state capital of Texas?
2. Which community is larger, Sarita or Del Rio? San Antonio or Beaumont?
3. Is Hereford in the northern or southern part of the state?
4. In what direction would you travel to go from Austin to Junction?

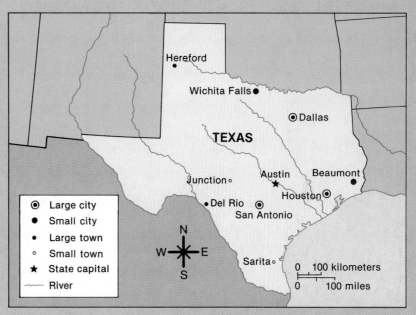

—————Your Community—————

Almost everyone lives in a community. Most people live in communities because they need each other. Everyone in the community tries to work together to supply the goods and services that the other people in the community need.

What goods and services do you need from your community? What goods and services can you supply?

UNIT 2

Our First Communities

Some of the communities in this country are very old. They were built by people who lived a long time ago. What was life in these communities like? Do you think that these communities are the same today?

In this unit, you will learn about some of the oldest communities in our country. You will find out what these communities were like long ago. You will also read about many changes that have taken place in these communities, and some things that have stayed the same.

CHAPTER 3 Shungopovi—Then and Now

Walpi, a modern Hopi village in Arizona

"Hopituh" (**hope**-ih-tuh) means "the peaceful ones." It is an American Indian word. From the word "Hopituh" comes the name "Hopi" (**hoe**-pee). The Hopi Indians have lived in Arizona for hundreds of years. In this chapter, you will learn about Shungopovi (shung-**oe**-poe-vee), a Hopi community.

At the end of this chapter, you should be able to:
○ Locate Shungopovi on a map.
● Read a diagram of landforms.
○ Describe Shungopovi's past.
○ Explain how Shungopovi has changed.

1 The Land of the Hopi Indians

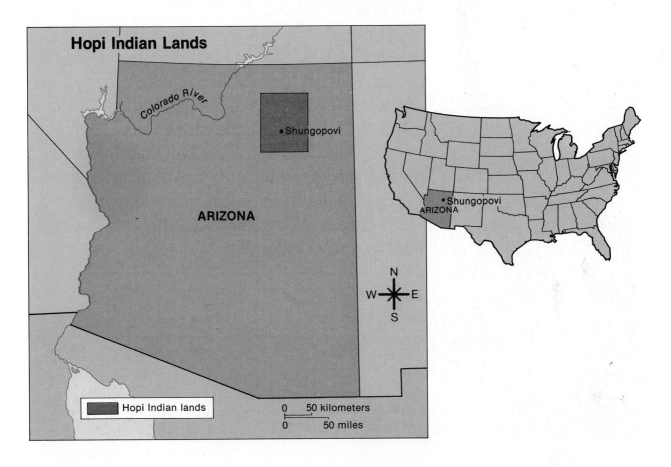

Hopi Indian Lands

Colorado River

•Shungopovi

ARIZONA

N W E S

Hopi Indian lands

0   50 kilometers
0   50 miles

•Shungopovi
ARIZONA

The map on this page shows the area where the Hopi live. It is in northeastern Arizona, east of the Colorado River. Find Shungopovi on the map.

Very little rain falls in this part of the United States. The sun shines almost every day. This kind of dry area is a good home for coyotes, rattlesnakes, and cacti. These animals and plants can live without much water.

This is a very beautiful land. It is not an easy place for people to live. But the Hopi Indians understand the land and have chosen it to be their home.

mesa
land with steep sides
and a flat top

arroyo
a ditch formed by flood
water

The community of Shungopovi is high on top of a **mesa** (**may**-suh). A mesa has steep sides and a flat top. The word "mesa" means "table" in Spanish.

The weather in northeastern Arizona has shaped the land in beautiful and special ways. You never have to walk far to find an **arroyo** (uh-**roi**-oe). An arroyo is a ditch formed by flood water. During a storm, the rain comes down hard and fast. Instead of soaking into the dry ground, the rainwater runs downhill. This flood water carries dirt and sticks and even small plants with it. The water wears the land down until an arroyo is formed.

Shungopovi, 1901

There are deep **canyons** in this part of the country. Canyons are narrow valleys with steep sides or walls. Some canyons are hundreds of meters deep.

This land of mesas, arroyos, and canyons is where the Hopi have lived and worked for hundreds of years.

canyon
a narrow valley with steep sides

Section Review

Write your answers on a sheet of paper.
1. What plants and animals live around Shungopovi?
2. How are arroyos formed?
3. Describe the shape of a mesa.
4. In what ways is the land where you live different from the Hopi land?

Reading a Diagram of Landforms

landform

the shape of an area of land

Because maps are usually drawn on paper, the land they show looks flat. But you know that the land around Shungopovi is not flat. This land has mesas, canyons, and arroyos. The shapes that land can take are called **landforms.**

The chart on this page tells about different landforms. Some landforms, such as mesas, are high places. Others are low places.

Use the pictures and sentences on the chart to find the high places. How many high places did you find? Which landforms are low places? Which landform on the chart can be either high or low?

Landforms	
MOUNTAIN	A **mountain** has steep slopes and is large and high. Some mountains are so high that their tops are covered with snow all year round.
HILL	A **hill** also has sides that slope. But hills are not as steep or high as mountains.
PLATEAU	A **plateau** is a high, flat stretch of land that is much larger than a mesa. Plateaus are sometimes called tablelands because of their flat tops.
PLAIN	A **plain** is an area of flat, open land. Plains are usually low places but there are also high plains.
VALLEY	A **valley** is a low place that lies between hills or mountains. Many valleys have rivers or streams flowing through them.
CANYON	A **canyon** is a narrow valley. It has high, steep sides that look almost like walls. Often a stream or river flows at the bottom of a canyon.

Imagine that you made a model of mountains and a valley out of clay. Then you took a knife and sliced the model in two the long way. What you have made is a cutaway model showing these landforms.

The same type of cutaway model can be shown on a diagram. The diagram below shows high and low places in the western United States. The highest mountains are shown in brown. Coastal mountains, plateaus, mesas, and hills are shown in yellow. The plains are shown in green. What color is used to show the valleys?

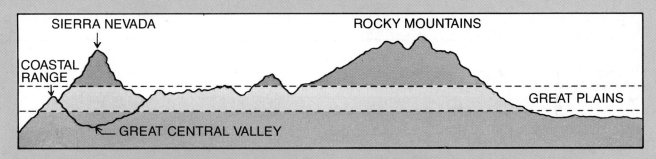

SIERRA NEVADA — ROCKY MOUNTAINS — COASTAL RANGE — GREAT PLAINS — GREAT CENTRAL VALLEY

═══ Practice Your Skills ═══

1. Which area on the cutaway is the highest?
2. Which area on the cutaway is the lowest?
3. Is the Central Valley area higher or lower than the Great Plains?
4. What mountain areas are shown on the cutaway?

2 Shungopovi Long Ago

The story of Shungopovi began about 1,000 years ago. At that time, the Hopi built their houses at the base of the mesa. Then, in 1680, Shungopovi was in danger of being attacked. The whole community moved to the top of the mesa. There they were safe.

Hopi women built the walls of their new homes out of stones. They used mud to hold the stones together and fill up any cracks. The men cut logs for the roofs. Across the logs they laid small poles, reeds, and twigs. Then a thick layer of earth was packed down to finish the roof.

To enter a house, a person first had to climb up a ladder to the roof. There, through a hole in the roof, was another ladder to climb down into the house. If the village was attacked, people pulled up the ladders. This made the community like a fort.

Shungopovi, 1940

Grinding corn in a Hopi pueblo, 1895

Modern Hopi blanket weaver

The homes of the Hopi were simple. In a corner was a fireplace used to heat the room in winter. Clay pots were used for cooking and for holding water. Men wove cotton blankets, which the Hopi used while sleeping. Hanging from the ceiling was a pole. The whole family hung their clothes on it.

As a Hopi family grew, more rooms were added to the house. The Hopi built rooms one on top of the other, until most of the buildings were three stories high. These houses are called **pueblos** (poo-**eb**-loes). The Spanish called all the Indians who built houses like this Pueblo Indians.

pueblo
an Indian house built of mud and stone

Kachina dance

kachina
a Hopi Indian spirit

For as long as the Hopi can remember, they have planted corn. Early in the morning, men and boys walked down the mesa to the fields. They planted and weeded the corn.

The Hopi asked spirits called **kachinas** (kah-**chee**-nahz) for rain to water the corn. They also asked the kachinas to bring joy and health to their people. On special days, some of the men put on kachina masks and painted themselves to look as they believed the spirits looked. They danced and shook rattles.

While the dancers danced, clowns played jokes. Their job was to make people laugh. This was a hard thing to do if there had been no rain and people were worried about the corn crop.

The kachina dance is part of the Hopi Way. The Hopi Way is how Hopi men and women think and act. It is the way the Hopi Indians have always lived.

To live the Hopi Way, a person does not pray only for himself or herself, or the community, or even the Hopi people. The Hopi Way is to pray for the whole earth. Why do you think the Hopi feel this way?

Kachina doll

Section Review

Write your answers on a sheet of paper.

1. Why are the Hopi people called Pueblo Indians?
2. With what materials did the Hopi build their homes?
3. What are kachinas?
4. In what ways is weather important in your life? Is it more or less important to you than to the Hopi?

3 Shungopovi Today

People in Shungopovi today still believe in the Hopi Way. The community gathers to watch the kachinas dance and to laugh at the clowns.

Other things in Shungopovi have changed. There are many reasons why this is so. In 1540, people from Spain came to the Hopi land. They claimed the land for their country. The Spanish brought guns and horses with them. They also brought peach trees, almond trees, sheep, and many other things.

After many years passed, a railroad was built through the Hopi land. It brought new people who came to make their homes on the land. These people are called **settlers.** The settlers brought jobs. Working for money was new to the Hopi.

settler
a person who comes to make a home in a place

Today, many of the Hopi have jobs in Shungopovi and in nearby towns. Some are teachers, and some work in stores or banks. Others are nurses, electricians, and plumbers.

Some of the Hopi people stay in Shungopovi and make things to sell. They make beautiful clay pots and silver jewelry. People from around the world come to buy Hopi goods.

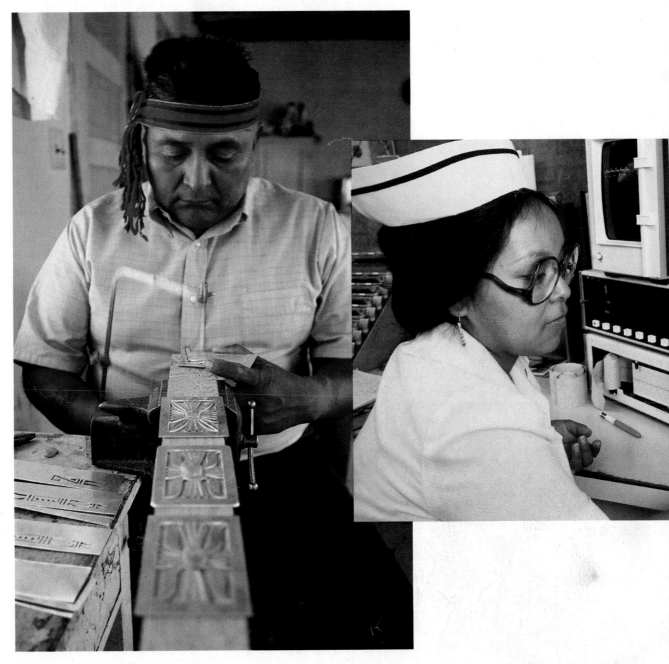

You can see many things in the picture on this page. The picture shows how the Hopi community has changed. There are roads, cars, and telephone poles. Now the houses have doors and glass windows.

You can also see things that have not changed. The houses are made of the same kind of stone and mud that was used long ago.

Many Hopi men and women want to keep some of the old ways. They want to keep things the way they have been for hundreds of years. The grown-ups teach their children the Hopi Way.

Section Review

Write your answers on a sheet of paper.
1. Name two ways Shungopovi has changed.
2. Name two ways Shungopovi has stayed the same.
3. Why do you think the Hopi teach their children the Hopi Way?

FAMOUS AMERICANS

MARÍA MARTÍNEZ

The Pueblo Indians are well-known for their beautiful clay pottery. One of the most famous Pueblo Indian potters was María Martínez. María learned how to make clay pots when she was about as old as you are now.

María Martínez lived at San Ildefonso (sahn il-day-**fahn**-soe) Pueblo. She learned how to make clay pottery by watching her aunt. She sat for hours and watched how each step was done. Soon María wanted to make pots by herself. It was not long before everyone in the pueblo knew of María and her wonderful clay pots.

Once María learned how to make pots, she never stopped. After María married, she and her husband, Julian, worked together. María made the pots and Julian painted them. He used very old Pueblo designs.

In 1911, María and Julian discovered something new to do to their pottery. They found that if they put the clay in a very hot fire, the pots would come out black and shiny.

Soon people all over the world heard about María and her pottery. María and Julian went to fairs and art shows. People paid high prices for their pottery.

María Martínez taught her children and her grandchildren how to make beautiful pottery. To this day, they have continued the wonderful work that she started.

CHAPTER 4

Santa Fe— Then and Now

The pictures on this page show some of the people who live in Santa Fe (**san**-tuh **fay**), New Mexico, today. In this chapter, you will learn about the people of Santa Fe and why they came to this city. You will learn about the people of Santa Fe long ago and how they have shaped the city of today.

At the end of this chapter, you should be able to:
- ◎ Describe the climate of Santa Fe and the area called the Southwest.
- ◉ Name two things that changed Santa Fe.
- ● Read a landmark map.
- ○ Name three different kinds of culture in Santa Fe.

1 Land of the Sun

Find Santa Fe on the map. Now put your finger in the middle of the United States. As you move your finger toward Santa Fe, in what direction is your finger moving? Look at the compass rose. Your finger moves south and west at the same time.

The part of the United States that is to the south and west is called the Southwest. Name two states in the Southwest. In what state is Santa Fe?

The Southwest has a sunny, dry **climate.** Climate is what the weather is usually like in a place over a long period of time. In sunny New Mexico, the *zia* (**zee**-uh), an American Indian sign for the sun, is on the state flag.

New Mexico state flag

climate
what the weather of an area is usually like over a long period of time

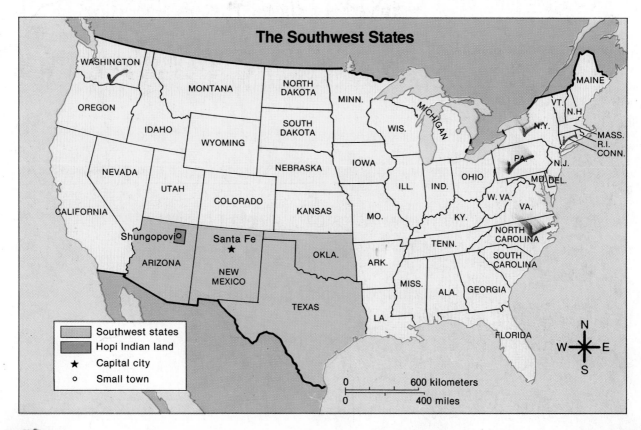

The Southwest States

- Southwest states
- Hopi Indian land
- ★ Capital city
- ○ Small town

0 — 600 kilometers
0 — 400 miles

Camel Rock, New Mexico

Just as the climate helped to shape the landforms around Shungopovi, the wind and weather have helped to shape the land around Santa Fe. Northern New Mexico, like northeastern Arizona, is a land of arroyos, mesas, mountains, and canyons.

Sometimes the wind and weather carve the rocks into odd shapes. The rock in the picture above is near Santa Fe. Why do you think this rock is called Camel Rock?

Section Review

Write your answers on a sheet of paper.
1. New Mexico is in what part of the United States?
2. Name three landforms found in northern New Mexico.
3. How do you think the climate in Santa Fe affects the way the people in this area live?

2 The Land and Its Past

Long ago, most of the Southwest belonged to American Indians and then to Spain. In 1610, the Spanish governor was Governor Peralta (puh-**rawl**-tuh). He wanted to build a capital city from which he could govern the Southwest.

The governor needed a place with fresh water and good soil to grow food. The capital had to be near the American Indian trails of the area. The Indian trails were the only way people could get from community to community.

After a short search, the governor found the right place. The spot had once been an Indian village. It lay at the bottom of snowcapped mountains. A clear stream flowed nearby. The American Indian trails were close and the soil was rich. This was the right place to begin building Santa Fe.

adobe
brick made of mud and chopped straw

Governor Peralta's government was located in the first building finished in Santa Fe. The building is called the Palace of the Governors.

The palace walls are built of **adobe** (uh-**doe**-bee) bricks. These bricks are made from mud and chopped straw. The bricks bake in the hot sun until they are hard.

Adobe bricks are large and heavy. They make thick walls. These thick walls keep houses warm in the winter and cool in the summer.

trader
a person who buys and sells goods

As soon as the capital was built, the first **traders** made the long trip from Mexico to Santa Fe. Traders are people who buy and sell goods.

Spanish and Mexican settlers also came to the new capital. They traveled in wagons pulled by horses or oxen.

The Palace of the Governors, Santa Fe, 1885

Making adobe bricks

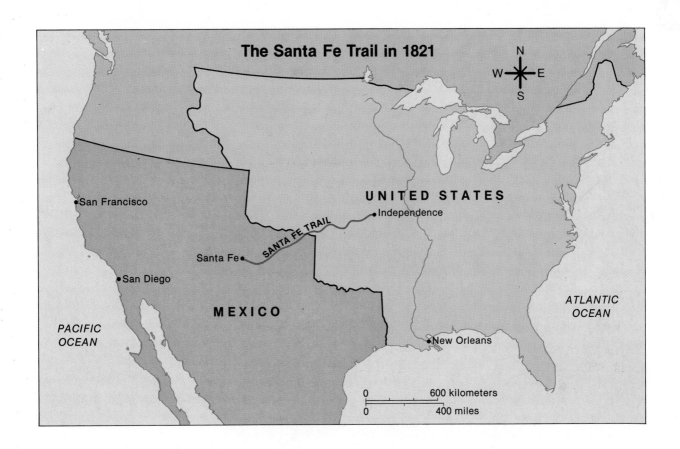

The Santa Fe Trail in 1821

The Spanish government in Santa Fe would not let traders from the United States come to their community. Then, in 1821, the Southwest and Mexico won their independence from Spain. The Southwest became part of independent Mexico. Now the flag of Mexico flew over the Palace of the Governors.

The new government in Santa Fe wanted to trade with the United States. The people of the Southwest needed many goods. The traders from the East could bring them.

The first trader from the United States to arrive in Santa Fe was William Becknell. He started his trip in Independence, Missouri. Becknell traveled to Santa Fe with many goods to sell to people in the West. With no roads to follow, his journey must have been long and difficult.

The end of the Santa Fe Trail

The next traders followed William Becknell's route. Soon there were many tracks along the route, and the way became known as the Santa Fe Trail.

Settlers also began to travel on the Santa Fe Trail. These people were moving to make new homes in the West.

The Santa Fe Trail was 1,260 kilometers (782 miles) long. Most people traveled the trail in large covered wagons pulled by oxen. The trip by wagon took many months.

The trip along the trail was long and dangerous. But settlers and traders kept coming. For over 50 years, the Santa Fe Trail was crowded with wagons bringing goods and people west. Santa Fe became a center of trade.

In 1880, a railroad reached Santa Fe. Trains were a much faster and safer way for people and goods to travel.

New communities began to grow around the railroads. The Santa Fe Trail was used less and less. Soon the trail was part of the past.

Section Review

Write your answers on a sheet of paper.

1. What materials were the first buildings in Santa Fe made of?
2. How did the Santa Fe Trail change Santa Fe?
3. Why did people stop using the Santa Fe Trail?
4. Name one change you think the railroads brought to Santa Fe.

Reading a Landmark Map

landmark

a building, statue, or place that is important or interesting

People often go to cities such as Santa Fe to visit interesting places. How do they find their way around in an unfamiliar city? One way is to ask questions. Another way is to use a **landmark** map.

A landmark map shows roads and streets. It also shows places of interest. Symbols such as these are often used to show important buildings and landmarks.

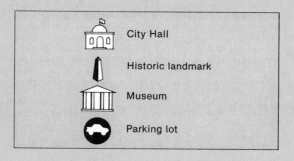

City Hall

Historic landmark

Museum

Parking lot

Find the symbol used to show a parking lot. Why might a visitor be interested in knowing this symbol?

To make things easy to find, a landmark map can be divided into boxes. Each box may have its own letter or number. This kind of system is called a grid.

The grid helps you look at the right area. It is faster to find a place in one box than in the whole map.

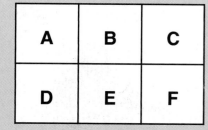

Look at the landmark map of Santa Fe. Find the box marked D. How many landmarks are found in this box? One symbol tells you that a parking lot is found in box D. Use the map key to find out what the other landmarks are.

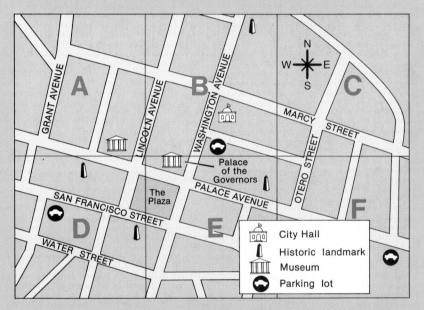

Practice Your Skills

1. What landmarks appear in box E?
2. In which boxes are the parking lots found?
3. If someone asked you where historical landmarks are found on the map, what would you say?
4. A convention center will be built next to City Hall. In which box would you put it on the map?

3 Santa Fe Today

Santa Fe today is both old and new. The Palace of the Governors is still on the open square, or **plaza,** in the city. The marker at the end of the Santa Fe Trail is also there. Today, though, the trail is gone. It is covered by streets and highways, fields and houses. The government is no longer located in the Palace of the Governors. But Santa Fe is still the capital city for the land around it. Today, that land is called New Mexico, and it is part of the United States.

plaza

an open square in a town or city

The marker at the end of the Santa Fe Trail

New Mexico state capitol building

There are still many old Spanish buildings made of adobe in Santa Fe. They give the city a special look. The people of Santa Fe do not want new buildings to change the look of their city. Most new buildings are not made of adobe, but they are built in the Spanish southwestern style to look like the old buildings.

Santa Fe is still an important trading center in New Mexico. But the biggest business in this community is taking care of visitors who have traveled to Santa Fe to see the sights. These people are called **tourists.**

Many tourists like to walk through the oldest parts of town. They like to look at the old Spanish buildings. They can imagine what it was like to be a settler or trader finally arriving at the end of the Santa Fe Trail.

tourist
a visitor who comes to see the sights in a community

Museum of Fine Arts, Santa Fe (built 1917)

culture
the way of life of a group of people who share a past, customs, beliefs, art, and often language

Santa Fe is a city with three kinds of **culture,** American Indian, Spanish, and Anglo. A culture is the way of life of a group of people who share a past, customs, beliefs, art, and often language.

American Indians from many tribes live and work in Santa Fe. Different tribes may speak different languages. But Indian tribes may have the same culture in other ways.

Once a year, American Indians from all over the country come to Santa Fe to go to an Indian market. Indian artists show their jewelry, pottery, rugs, and paintings in the plaza. Visitors come to the Indian market from around the world. Some come just to look. Some come to buy the beautiful handmade things. For two days, the plaza is a center of trade again.

Indian Market, Santa Fe

The Spanish culture is another important culture in Santa Fe. One Spanish custom in Santa Fe today is the fiesta (fee-**es**-tah). A "fiesta" is a "holiday." People from far and near come to the plaza for dances and music. Around the plaza, booths are set up to serve New Mexican and American Indian food.

The third culture in Santa Fe is the Anglo culture. Most of the settlers and traders who came from the rest of the United States were Anglos. They were the only English-speaking people in the area. The Anglos brought their culture with them too.

American Indian, Spanish, and Anglo—these are the cultures that shape Santa Fe today.

Fiesta in Santa Fe

Section Review

Write your answers on a sheet of paper.
1. What are the three kinds of culture in Santa Fe?
2. Give an example of a Spanish custom.
3. List three things you think are part of your culture.

St. Augustine— Then and Now

Oldest house in St. Augustine, Florida

The picture on this page shows a house in the oldest city settled by Europeans in the United States. It is just one of the many famous old buildings in St. Augustine, Florida.

In this chapter, you will learn more about places to visit in St. Augustine. You will learn why settlers came to the area. You also will learn why people still visit St. Augustine.

At the end of this chapter, you should be able to:
○ Describe the landforms around St. Augustine.
○ Describe the climate of St. Augustine.
○ Tell who first settled the city and why these people settled in the area.
○ Name industries in St. Augustine today.

1 The Land at St. Augustine

Most of Florida is a **peninsula.** A peninsula is a piece of land almost entirely surrounded by water. The land around St. Augustine is part of a coastal plain. The city itself is located at the mouth of the Matanzas (muh-**tahn**-suhs) River.

There are many small islands, coral reefs, and sand bars along the Florida coast. An **island** is a body of land entirely surrounded by water. Coral reefs and sand bars are places where coral and sand build up under the water. The sea is shallow in these places. The Spanish people who explored the area had problems sailing their ships to the shore because of the coral reefs and sand bars. The large boats would hit the sea bottom in the shallow waters.

peninsula
land almost entirely surrounded by water

island
a body of land entirely surrounded by water

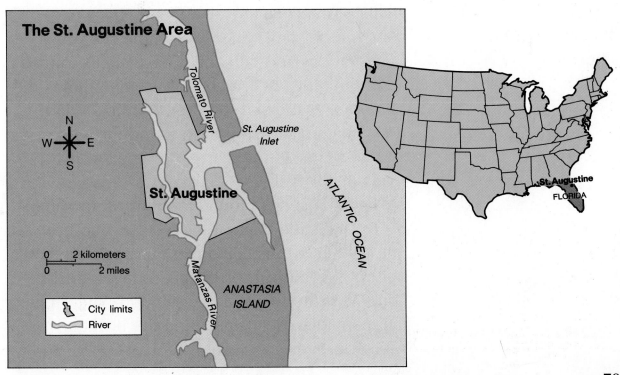

The St. Augustine Area

Tolomato River

St. Augustine Inlet

St. Augustine

ATLANTIC OCEAN

N W E S

0   2 kilometers
0   2 miles

Matanzas River

ANASTASIA ISLAND

City limits
River

St. Augustine
FLORIDA

Coquina quarry, Anastasia Island

coquina
a kind of stone made of the broken shells of many small sea animals

humid
damp

Look at the map on page 79. Find the St. Augustine Inlet. The Spanish found that small ships could get through this inlet to land. They thought that the waters west of the inlet would make a safe harbor. So they decided that this was a good place for a settlement.

A harbor is one kind of natural resource. The Spanish found another important resource on Anastasia (ah-nuh-**stah**-zee-uh) Island. This resource is called **coquina** (koe-**kee**-nuh). Coquina is a kind of stone made of the broken shells of many small sea animals. Long ago, some of the shells dissolved in the sea water that then covered the land. These shells formed a kind of glue, or cement. The cement holds the other pieces of shell together, forming a hard, rocky material. The Spanish found that coquina was good for building. It is still used to make roads and buildings.

The early settlers found that the warm climate of St. Augustine made it a good place to live. The winters are usually mild. Summers are hot but not too **humid,** or damp. Today, tourists come to visit the city all year round. They enjoy the many historical sights and the beautiful sandy beaches.

St. Augustine does have hurricanes, though. A **hurricane** is a storm with rain and very strong winds. These storms usually occur in late summer and fall. St. Augustine and the land around it are not very high above the sea. Because the land is so low, the winds of a hurricane can blow huge waves far up onto the shore. St. Augustine has been flooded during several hurricanes.

hurricane
a storm with rain and very strong winds

Section Review

Write your answers on a sheet of paper.
1. On what kind of landform is St. Augustine?
2. How is coquina used?
3. At what time of year would you like to visit St. Augustine? Why?

2 Early Days in an Old City

In the 1500's, Spain had many colonies in North and South America. A **colony** is a place settled by people from another country and still ruled by that country. The Spanish had started these colonies in order to bring home gold and other riches from the Americas. When explorers landed in a new place, they claimed the land for the king or queen of their country. Florida was part of the land claimed by Spanish explorers for the king of Spain.

In 1562, a group of French people started a settlement in Florida. The king of Spain did not want people from other countries on his land. He sent Pedro Menéndez de Avilés (**pay**-droe meh-**nen**-dez day ah-vee-**lays**) to Florida to drive the French away. Menéndez landed in Florida on June 28, 1565. He came with soldiers and ships, and drove the French from Florida. He also brought people and supplies to start a new settlement. He named the settlement St. Augustine because June 28 is that saint's day.

*American Indians in Florida
meet the Spanish explorers*

A map of St. Augustine in 1586

Though Menéndez had driven the French from Florida, the Spanish there still had troubles. More and more trading ships from Spain, England, and France were sailing up and down the coast. Pirates from other countries attacked Spanish ships and settlements. Soldiers from St. Augustine did what they could to protect Spanish lands and trading ships.

In 1586 an English sea captain, Sir Francis Drake, captured St. Augustine. He burned it down and destroyed the crops. But the Spanish did not give up. They built the town again.

By 1650, the English had settlements of their own in the lands north of Florida. In 1668 another English sea captain, Robert Searles, raided St. Augustine. Then the English started another settlement that was even closer to Florida than were their earlier ones. The Spanish became very worried about the English.

The Spanish decided they needed a stronger fort. The wooden ones burned easily, or rotted away. In 1672, they started building a fort made of coquina from Anastasia Island. The fort was named Castillo de San Marcos (kah-**stee**-yoe day san **mar**-kos). The new stone fort helped them defend their town.

St. Augustine may have looked like this in colonial times.

The Spanish still had problems in places other than Florida. Spain and England went to war in 1762. England captured Havana, Cuba. Cuba is an island near Florida. It was Spain's most important colony in the New World. To get Havana back, Spain gave Florida to England. Spanish people left St. Augustine at this time and went to live in Cuba.

Another war, called the American Revolution, started in 1775. This war was fought between England and the English colonies in North America. The English colonies won the war and started a new nation, the United States. At this time, eastern Florida still belonged to England. Many people who did not want to live in the United States came to Florida. The English decided it was too hard to find food, housing, and jobs for all these people. So they gave Florida back to Spain and left. Spanish people came back to live in St. Augustine.

The Spanish had a lot of trouble ruling Florida. Finally, in 1819, Spain signed a treaty with the United States. From then on, Florida belonged to the United States.

Section Review

Write your answers on a sheet of paper.
1. Why did Menéndez come to Florida?
2. Why did the Spanish in St. Augustine need to defend themselves?
3. What made Castillo de San Marcos better than the old forts?

3 St. Augustine Today

The first settlers in St. Augustine came from Spain. Many were from the small island of Minorca. There are still people in St. Augustine who are related to the Spanish from Minorca. But there are many others whose families came from other parts of Europe, or from Africa. Many people have recently come to St. Augustine from Cuba. Others have moved to St. Augustine from colder parts of the United States.

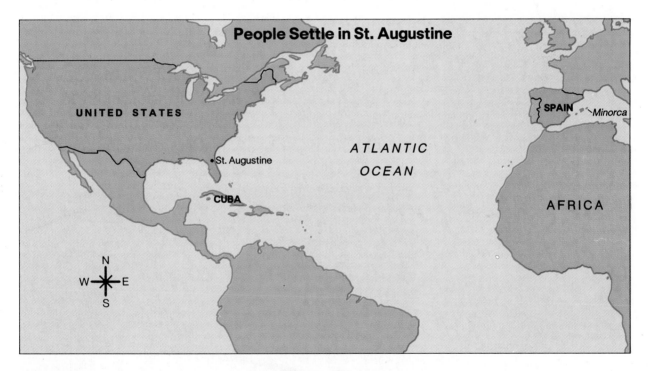

People Settle in St. Augustine

Retired people have come here to enjoy the warm climate. But many people have worked and lived in St. Augustine all their lives. There are people who fish for shrimp, mackerel, mullet, and other fish along the coast. Small factories in the area make boats and fishing rods and reels. These are used for fishing around St. Augustine and in other parts of Florida.

quarry

a place where stone is cut or blasted out of the ground

Making crafts as they were made in colonial times (above) A lantern maker (right) A weaver

There is also a coquina industry in St. Augustine. Workers dig coquina out of quarries on nearby Anastasia Island. A **quarry** is a place where stone is cut or blasted out of the ground. The coquina is still used for building houses and garden walls, as it was in earlier times.

Most of the people of St. Augustine work in businesses that take care of tourists. Many visitors come to St. Augustine to enjoy the fine weather and the beaches. The people of the town run the many hotels, motels, parks, and restaurants.

Other people work at taking care of the old buildings in St. Augustine. Many houses, shops, churches, and gardens have been rebuilt to look like they did in the early days. Even a school and a jail have been rebuilt to look like old Spanish buildings. Local workers make things in the old shops, just as workers did long ago.

Castillo de San Marcos, St. Augustine

Visitors can learn about the crafts of colonial times. They can watch the work being done, and ask questions of the workers. Visitors can still feel what it was like to walk through the streets and gardens of a Spanish settlement. They can also see the Spanish fort of Castillo de San Marcos. It is the oldest stone fort in the United States. It faced many raids and attacks, but its strong coquina walls were never broken down. Like much of St. Augustine, it keeps the past alive for all to see.

Section Review

Write your answers on a sheet of paper.
1. What island did many of the first settlers of St. Augustine come from?
2. What jobs do people in St. Augustine do today?
3. What type of buildings in St. Augustine have been rebuilt to look as they did long ago?
4. How do the people of St. Augustine help keep its past alive for visitors?

6 Plymouth— Then and Now

The time was December in the year 1620. A small ship appeared off the east coast of North America. The ship had been at sea for 65 days. The people aboard were hungry, tired, and sick.

The name of the ship was the *Mayflower.* The people it carried called themselves the Pilgrims. They had come to America from England to begin a new community.

At the end of this chapter, you should be able to:

○ Define the term "bay."

● Use the distance scale on a map.

○ Explain who the Pilgrims were.

○ Explain why people remember Plymouth today.

● Read a family-history chart.

1 The Land at Plymouth

Communities begin in places where people can use the natural resources. The people on the *Mayflower* knew that they needed good farmland and fresh water. They needed a place that was safe too.

After the Pilgrims arrived in North America, they sent a scouting party to explore the area near the coast. Everyone else stayed on board the ship. Within a month, the scouts found a place they liked. There was a steep hill, which could protect the new community. The scouts found brooks of fresh water. Nearby was flat land, where crops could be planted. And the place was near the sea, so ships bringing supplies could land. The Pilgrims called their new community Plymouth.

Wood for building houses could be cut from the nearby forests. Near the shore, the settlers found sand. The sand could be used for building, too. The settlers also found some clay. What do you think the settlers made with it?

The settlement at Plymouth, 1621

PLYMOUTH HARBOR

ATLANTIC OCEAN

The Mount

The little field that overlooks the Sea

The Landing Rock

The Ship

Shallop

Spring

The Inlet

The Brook

Footlog

Deer Trail

Governor's Rock

Look at the map on this page. Plymouth is located on a body of water. Look at the shape of this body of water. It is partly surrounded by land. A body of water partly surrounded by land is called a **bay.** Bays are good harbors.

On the map, find the ocean near Plymouth. What larger bay is Plymouth Bay near?

The map also shows you where the *Mayflower* first landed. Today, this place is called Provincetown. The Pilgrims landed at the tip of a long strip of land now known as Cape Cod. The scouts explored most of Cape Cod before finding Plymouth.

bay
a body of water partly surrounded by land

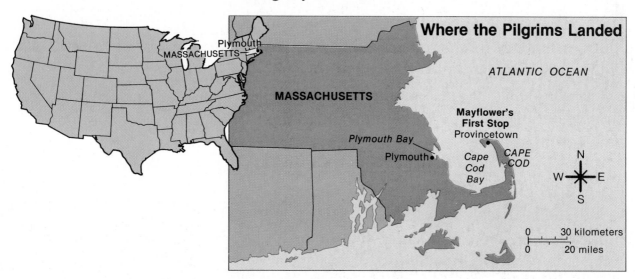

Where the Pilgrims Landed

Section Review

Write your answers on a sheet of paper.
1. Name two natural resources the Pilgrims needed to begin their new community.
2. Name three natural resources the Pilgrims found at Plymouth.
3. Why do you think a bay makes a good harbor?

Determining Size on a Map

The maps on this page show the United States, Massachusetts, and Plymouth. The three maps are about the same size. Are the places shown on the maps the same size?

Massachusetts is only one state. It must be smaller than all of the United States. You know that Plymouth is a town in the state of Massachusetts. What does this tell you about the size of Plymouth compared to the size of Massachusetts?

If you had never heard of Massachusetts or Plymouth, how would you know which was bigger? To figure out the true size of a place on a map, you need to use the distance scale. Look at the distance scale for each map on this page.

On the United States map, one centimeter stands for 800 kilometers (480 miles) on the earth. On the map of Massachusetts, how many kilometers does one centimeter show?

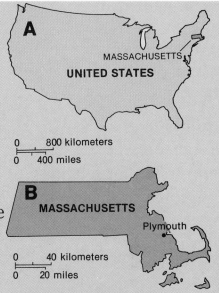

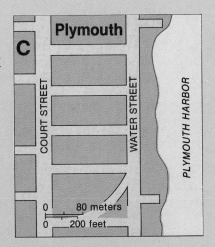

Practice Your Skills

1. Which map shows a larger area, A or C?
2. Which map shows a smaller area, B or A?
3. Which map shows an area that would take longer to drive across, B or C?

2 Pilgrim Life in Plymouth

The people on the *Mayflower* came to America from England because of their religious beliefs. In England, people were allowed to worship in only one way. People who had other religious ideas were punished.

The passengers on the *Mayflower* were called the Pilgrims. A **pilgrim** is a person who makes a trip, often for religious reasons. The Pilgrims left their homes and sailed to a land they hardly knew. They came to America to build a community where they could live and worship in their own way.

The trip to America was not easy. The *Mayflower* was very crowded. The children had no place to play. It was hard to find a place to sleep. Bad storms at sea made the trip even harder.

pilgrim
a person who makes a trip, often for religious reasons

The Pilgrims knew they had to work together or their new community would not last. Before the ship landed, the Pilgrims made an important agreement. The agreement was called the Mayflower Compact.

The signing of the Mayflower Compact

In the Mayflower Compact, the Pilgrims agreed to choose their own leaders and to obey just and equal laws. The agreement was important to the Pilgrims. It helped them set up their own government.

In England, people did not always vote for leaders or laws. The king often decided these things. In America, people would have leaders they elected. In America, people would live under laws they had helped to make.

wilderness
unsettled land

In 1620, Plymouth was an unsettled land, or **wilderness.** American Indians had lived there long ago, but sickness had wiped out the tribe at Plymouth. The Pilgrims found no Indians in the place chosen by their scouts. There were no roads, stores, or schools in the area. There were no offices or factories. There were no cities or towns. The Pilgrims had to begin their own community.

The first months in America were very hard for the Pilgrims. The winter in Plymouth was cold. The frozen ground was hard to dig. Sickness spread through the community. Nearly half of the Pilgrims died.

By March, some people began to lose hope. Then, all of a sudden, the Pilgrims had a big surprise. A tall American Indian came to Plymouth.

His name was Samoset (**sahm**-oe-set). Samoset had learned English from sea captains who sailed along the coast.

Samoset welcomes the Pilgrims.

94

Trade between the Pilgrims and the Wampanoag Indians

Soon Samoset brought another visitor to Plymouth. His name was Squanto (**skwahn**-toe).

Squanto showed the Pilgrims how to catch eels and fish. He showed them how to prepare the soil and plant corn. He also knew what plants to use for medicines.

One day, Squanto brought Ousamequin (oo-sah-**may**-kwin) to meet the Pilgrims. Ousamequin was a Massasoit (mass-uh-**soy**-it), or great leader of the Wampanoag (wahm-puh-**noe**-ag) Indians who lived nearby. Ousamequin and the Pilgrims became friends. Sometimes they traded things. In return for furs, the Pilgrims gave the Wampanoags cloth, lace, copper chains, knives, and food.

A Pilgrim kitchen might have looked like this.

With the help of the American Indians, things began to get better for the Pilgrims. The warm spring sun helped make them healthy again. They planted corn, barley, peas, squash, and beans. Soon these crops began to grow.

The Pilgrims finished building their houses. Each house had one large room with a fireplace at one end. Paper dipped in oil was used instead of glass in the windows.

The most important building in the new community was the Common House. The Pilgrims went there to worship every Sunday. They held town meetings there too.

That fall, the Pilgrims had a good harvest. They planned a big feast to give thanks. Men hunted wild turkeys, geese, and ducks. They caught lobsters, clams, and fish. Children picked plums, grapes, and wild berries. The women prepared all the food.

Ousamequin and other members of his tribe came to join the Pilgrims' feast. The Wampanoag Indians and the Pilgrims gave thanks for the fine meal they shared together. They gave thanks for the good harvest. Most of all, the Pilgrims gave thanks for the success of their tiny new community. This feast was called Harvest Home by the Pilgrims. It has come to be known as America's first Thanksgiving.

The first Thanksgiving at Plymouth, Massachusetts

In 1621, the Pilgrims chose William Bradford as governor of the new community. Governor Bradford worked hard for the new settlement. He helped the Pilgrims for the next 30 years. During these years, Governor Bradford wrote a book. It told about Plymouth. In his book, William Bradford wrote these words: "As one small candle may light a thousand, so the light kindled [burned] here has shone unto . . . our whole nation."

Think about Governor Bradford's words. They are his way of saying that the Plymouth community was an important beginning for our nation.

(above) William Bradford

(right) Plymouth, Massachusetts probably looked like this in the 1620's.

Section Review

Write your answers on a sheet of paper.
1. Why was the Mayflower Compact important?
2. Name two problems that the Pilgrims faced when they first landed at Plymouth.
3. Why did the Pilgrims hold a feast?
4. Why do you think we remember the Pilgrims' harvest feast today?

Reading a Family-History Chart

You know that your grandparents are the parents of your parents. Did you know that your grandparents also had grandparents? One way to remember their names is to make a family-history chart.

Peleg Bradford lived a long time ago. His great-great-great grandfather was the first governor of Massachusetts. A family-history chart for Peleg Bradford's family might look like this.

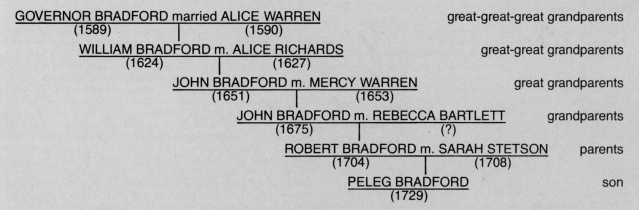

Peleg's name is at the bottom. Just above his name are his parents' names. The numbers under the names tell when the people were born. Find the names of Peleg's father's parents.

═══ Practice Your Skills ═══

1. When was Peleg born?
2. What were Peleg's parents' names?
3. Who was Peleg's great-great grandmother? In what year was she born?

3 Plymouth Today

Today, more than 19,000 people live in Plymouth. They work, play, and go to school.

Plymouth keeps growing. Many families have moved to Plymouth from larger cities. They come to Plymouth to have their own houses and more space for their children to play.

Look at the picture of Plymouth. You can tell from the picture that Plymouth is no longer a wilderness.

A woman in a Pilgrim costume, at Plimoth Plantation

Many people today work at Plimoth Plantation. "Plimoth" is the way the Pilgrims spelled Plymouth.

Plimoth Plantation is a village that was built to look like the Pilgrims' first community. In the harbor, visitors can see the *Mayflower II.* This ship looks like the one that carried the Pilgrims to America. People can visit Plymouth Rock. Stories say that the Pilgrims stepped on this rock when they first came ashore. Visiting the plantation is a good way to learn about Plymouth's past.

Today, people call Plymouth "America's Hometown." Why is that a good nickname for one of the first communities in the United States?

Plymouth Rock

Section Review

Write your answers on a sheet of paper.
1. What is Plimoth Plantation?
2. Name two places to visit in Plymouth today.
3. What would you like to learn about your community's past?

Close-up on

Square Dancing "All join hands! Circle to the left! Bow to your partner! And everybody swing!"

The caller taps a foot and gets ready to tell the dancers what steps to do. Lively music starts to play, and the square dance begins.

No one is sure where or when square dancing started. The idea may have come from England or France. But today, square dancing is known as the United States' own folk dance.

In the 1800's Americans loved to square dance. In those days, it was not easy to travel very far. Life in the country could be lonely. A barn dance was a good way to get together with friends and neighbors.

America

Sometimes dancers had to sprinkle water on a dirt floor to keep the dust down. Then four couples stood in a square. The caller picked up a fiddle, played the music, and called out directions for the dancers. Everyone followed the caller's directions.

In the early 1900's, Americans seemed to forget about square dancing. People did other kinds of

dances. Now square dancing has been remembered. Many people go to square dance festivals and contests.

Today, men and women join square-dance clubs, where they learn new square dances. They also make new friends. Everyone likes to dress up in bright colors and listen to the lively music that is always played at square dances.

UNIT REVIEW

Word Work

Write the sentences below on a sheet of paper. Fill in the blanks with the correct words from the list.

climate   peninsula   settlers   bay

1. A ___ is land almost surrounded by water.
2. A ___ is a body of water partly surrounded by land.
3. What the weather is like in a place over a long period of time is called the ___.
4. ___ are people who come to make their homes in a new place.

Knowing the Facts

Write your answers on a sheet of paper.

1. How did the Hopi Indians build their homes?
2. What three cultures are part of Santa Fe today?
3. What made the Pilgrims' first year so hard?
4. Who were the first settlers in St. Augustine?

Using What You Know

1. Ask someone in your family to help you make a family-history chart. Include your great-grandparents on the chart.
2. Write a short letter to a friend telling why you would like to visit one of the communities you have just read about.

Skills Practice

Use the following landmark map and map key to answer the questions below. Write your answers on a sheet of paper.

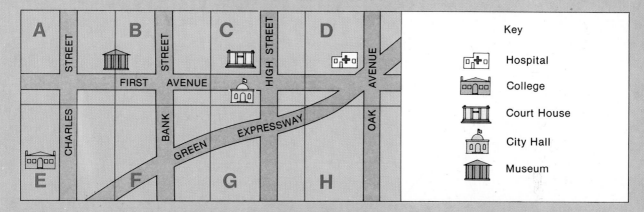

1. What landmark appears in box D?
2. Which box contains two landmarks?
3. In which box do Oak Avenue, First Avenue, and the Green Expressway cross?
4. If you were walking from the museum to the hospital, what route would you take?

Your Community

Many people are proud to remember special times in the history of their community. Some communities have festivals. Others may have special parades. Most communities remember the many women and men who first settled their communities. What special times does your community remember?

UNIT
3
Communities Are Centers of Work

The goods and services a community provides and uses may depend on the natural resources that are nearby. A community that is near good farmland may produce food. A community that has a pleasant climate may provide services for vacationers. In this unit, you will learn about five communities and the goods and services that each provides.

7 Pella—
A Farming Community

Pella (**pel**-uh) is a farming community in the state of Iowa. Many people in the Pella area are farmers. They grow corn or raise cattle and hogs. Many other jobs in Pella also have something to do with farming. Some people make farm machines. Others supply goods and services needed by farmers.

At the end of this chapter, you should be able to:
○ Name the natural resources important to a farming community.
● Interpret a picture graph.
○ Explain how Pella began and how it remembers its past.
○ Describe the work of farming in Pella.

1 Land for Farming

Pella is an important farming community. Farming, or **agriculture,** is a big business in Iowa. Find Iowa on the map. You can see that Iowa is part of a big farming area in the United States. Sometimes people call Iowa the Corn State because so much corn is grown there.

Like most of Iowa, Pella is on the **prairie.** The prairie is flat or rolling land that was once covered with tall grass. The prairie has layers of rich soil. This earth is some of the best farming soil in the world.

Most of Iowa's rain falls between April and September, when crops are growing. This period of time is called the **growing season.** Rain is an important natural resource for a farming community.

Farmers in Iowa grow many farm products for the United States. Besides corn, Iowa grows soybeans, oats, hay, and wheat.

agriculture
the business of farming

prairie
flat or rolling land that was once covered with tall grass

growing season
the period of time when crops are growing

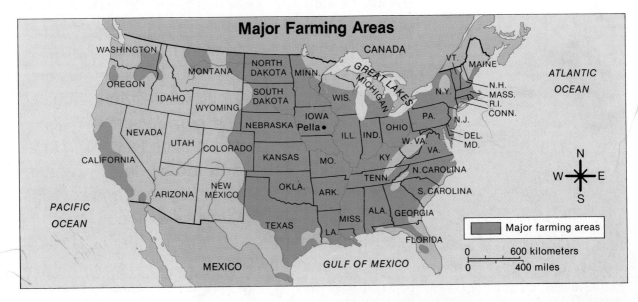

Major Farming Areas

(left) Looking at the sheep, Iowa State Fair   (right) Summer on the farm

Each season in Pella is very different. Winters are very cold. Lakes and ponds freeze. Snow covers the town and fields for many months.

Spring is an important season in Pella. Farmers work hard to get the corn planted. Spring is also the time when the community's gardens bloom with colorful tulips.

Summers in Pella are very hot. The town's parks and pools are busy. But hot summers are just right for corn. Corn grows best in a climate that has hot weather and rain. At summer's end, many people visit the Iowa State Fair. The fair is held in Des Moines (**duh moin**), Iowa's capital. At the fair, visitors look at farm machines, crops, and animals. Everyone enjoys the booths and carnival rides.

Fall is harvest time in a farming community. It is also the time to get ready for winter.

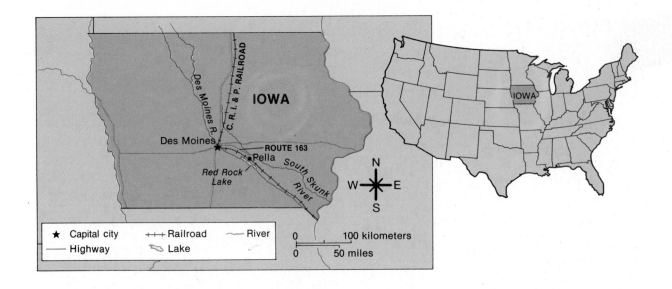

The maps tell you more about Pella. You can see that Pella is a long way from an ocean. But Pella is not very far from water. What lake and rivers are nearby?

Pella is near the capital city of Des Moines. A highway and a railroad link Pella with this city. **Transportation,** or ways of moving things from place to place, is important to a farming community. Farmers load their crops into trucks and railroad freight cars that carry them to markets where they are sold.

transportation
ways of moving things from place to place

Section Review

Write your answers on a sheet of paper.
1. Name two natural resources a farming community needs.
2. Describe the seasons in Pella.
3. How do seasons in Pella compare with seasons in your part of the United States?

Reading a Picture Graph

Pella, Iowa, has cold winters and hot summers. But how much rain falls there during the growing season? This **picture graph** shows you.

A picture graph is a chart that uses symbols to stand for information. Look at the picture graph below. What symbol is used to stand for one centimeter of rain?

picture graph
a chart that uses symbols to stand for information

To tell how much rain fell during July, find the word "July" under the "MONTH" heading. Then count the raindrop symbols next to the word "July." There are eight raindrops next to the word "July," so you know that eight centimeters of rain fell during that month.

Rainfall in Pella, Iowa	
MONTH	Centimeters of rain
April	◊◊◊◊◊
May	◊◊◊◊◊◊◊
June	◊◊◊
July	◊◊◊◊◊◊◊
August	◊◊◊◊◊◊◊◊◊◊◊◊◊◊◊◊◊◊
September	◊◊◊◊◊◊◊◊◊

Key: ◊ =1 centimeter of rain

Credit: Information on rainfall in Pella, Iowa, from April to September, 1977, courtesy of David Flikkema.

══ Practice Your Skills ══

1. Which month had the least rainfall?
2. Which month had the most rainfall?
3. How many centimeters of rain fell in September?
4. How many months had more rainfall than April had?

2 Pella's Past

Locate the Netherlands on the map. The first European settlers in Pella came from the Netherlands. People from the Netherlands are known as the Dutch.

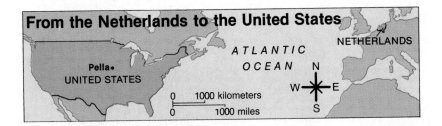

From the Netherlands to the United States

In the 1800's, some people were not happy in the Netherlands. They were allowed to worship in only one way. In 1847, a group of people decided to leave the Netherlands. Their leader was Henry Peter Scholte (**shol**-tuh). People called him Dominie (**dom**-uh-nee), which means "minister."

Dominie Scholte bought land in Iowa. He began a new community there. He called it Pella. In Pella, people could worship as they chose.

At first, people in Pella spoke Dutch. They wore Dutch clothes. But soon Dominie Scholte called the people of Pella together. They decided something important. They decided to become citizens of their new country, the United States.

Like settlers from many other countries, the Dutch people in Pella learned to speak English. They learned about their new government. They voted for its leaders. They became Americans.

The people of Pella are proud of their Dutch past. They are proud of the settlers who started their community. Part of the town has been set aside as a historical village to honor Pella's history. In this village, visitors can see some of Pella's first homes. They can also see an early barn, a mill for grinding corn, and old farm tools. The village shows what Pella looked like more than 135 years ago.

Scenes at the Pella Historical Village   (left) Grist mill   (right) Women in Dutch costumes

Section Review

Write your answers on a sheet of paper.

1. Why did some Dutch people leave the Netherlands in the 1800's?
2. What important thing did the early settlers in Pella decide?
3. Why do you think people in a community honor its history?

3 Pella Today

The first farmers in Pella had to work very hard to plow the soil. Today farmers still work hard. But they have modern tools and machines that make farming easier. Now farmers use machines to turn over the soil, plant the seeds, and harvest the crops.

Corn is an important crop in Pella. Most of the corn grown in Pella is not grown for people. It is used to feed farm animals such as cows, pigs, and chickens. The chart on this page shows many of the ways people use corn.

Hogs and cattle are also important to farmers in Iowa. Some farmers raise these animals for their meat. Other farmers raise dairy cows for their milk.

Feeding the pigs

Uses of Corn

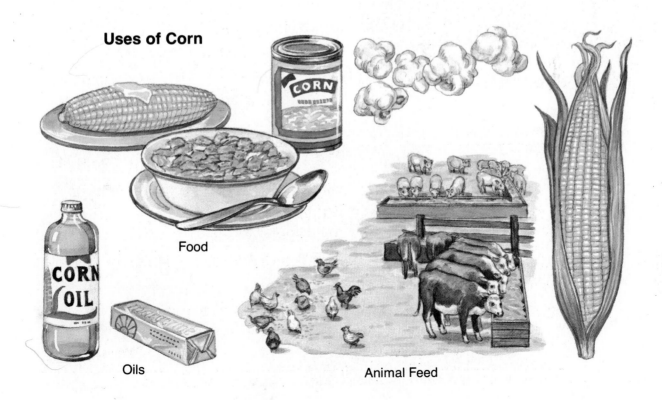

Food

Oils

Animal Feed

exchange
a place where people give and receive information or help

Today many farmers are learning new and better ways to farm. Some farmers in Pella belong to a farmer's **exchange.** This is a place where people give and receive information or help.

The exchange works with colleges and other groups to improve the agriculture of the community. Experts may test samples of a farmer's soil to see how to make it richer.

The exchange also studies new kinds of corn, and how to get rid of insects and diseases that attack corn. Through the exchange, farmers get low prices on feed for cattle and other things they need for farming.

Boys and girls in farm communities may join such clubs as Future Farmers of America or 4-H. The four *H*'s in 4-H stand for "head, heart, hands, and health." Both clubs have special programs for young farmers.

Members learn to can vegetables, raise animals, plant trees, and do many other things. They also work on projects to help the community. For example, 4-H'ers may work on programs to fight such problems as pollution.

Showing a prize sheep at the state fair

Making farm machines, Pella, Iowa

Not everyone in Pella is a farmer. Many people work in stores, schools, and banks in the community. People in Pella also work at making goods in factories or businesses. Producing things in factories or businesses is called **industry.**

A few companies in Pella make farm machines. Some of these are sold to farm communities around the United States. One such machine is called a baler. It helps farmers pick up and roll hay into bundles called bales.

Pella's biggest company makes windows and sliding doors. They are known all over the United States and in some foreign countries. Perhaps you can find a Pella window or door in a new building in your community.

industry
producing things in factories or businesses

117

About 8,000 people live in Pella. Farm children travel to the town center to go to school.

A community as small as Pella does not need a full-time fire department. Instead, it calls on volunteers if a fire breaks out. Pella does have a full-time police force. It includes nine people.

Pella has a mayor and city council. These leaders work to keep Pella clean and safe. The community is proud of its schools, parks, and other public buildings.

Marion County State Bank, Pella, Iowa

Tulips, Pella Tulip Festival

The leaders of Pella work to keep the feeling of the community's Dutch past. Many buildings have been rebuilt to have a Dutch look. One famous kind of Dutch building is a windmill. A windmill uses the energy of the wind to make machines go. A picture on page 118 shows a bank in Pella. It was built to look like a windmill.

Street scrubbing, Pella Tulip Festival

The Netherlands is famous for growing beautiful tulips. Each spring, Pella has a tulip festival. Visitors come to Pella to admire thousands of colorful tulips planted throughout the town. Visitors eat Dutch food such as pea soup, spiced beef, and cookies called Dutch letters. Many people join in the dancing and singing in the town square.

Visitors also enjoy a custom called street scrubbing. The people of Pella sweep and scrub the streets before the Tulip Time parade starts. For street scrubbing, most people wear bright Dutch costumes. They also wear *klompen,* which are wooden shoes.

Once the streets are clean, the parade begins. It is a special time in this community.

Section Review

Write your answers on a sheet of paper.
1. Besides corn, what do farmers in Pella raise?
2. Besides farming, what other kinds of work do people in Pella do?
3. Why do you think people in Pella have a tulip festival?

8 Thomasville—A Manufacturing Community

Communities are proud of the work their people do and the goods their people make. The big chair in the picture is in Thomasville, North Carolina. Thomasville is a community in the southeastern part of the United States. This town is a center for furniture making. In this chapter, you will learn about Thomasville.

At the end of this chapter, you should be able to:

○ Give two reasons why natural resources are important to a manufacturing community.

○ Tell why Thomasville began near a railroad route.

○ Explain how an industry may be important to a community.

1 Industry and Resources

The industry of a community may depend on the community's natural resources. Wood is a natural resource needed to make furniture. Many kinds of trees grow in the forests near Thomasville. This is why furniture making has become a main industry in Thomasville.

Thomasville's furniture is produced partly by people and partly by machines. Making a large number of products by machine is called **manufacturing.** The machines used in manufacturing need a source of power. In Thomasville, that power comes from a natural resource, water. North Carolina has many **dams,** or walls that control the flow of water in rivers. When water is released from dams, the power from the flow of the water is used to make electricity. Thomasville uses this electrical power to run the machines needed for manufacturing.

manufacturing
making a large number of products by machine

dam
a wall that controls the flow of water in a river

(left) Harvesting trees, Lumberton, North Carolina (right) Fontana Dam, North Carolina

The map on this page tells more about Thomasville. It shows where North Carolina is in the United States. Find Thomasville on the map. It is in the southern part of the United States.

Thomasville is near several other cities. These cities are in a part of the state called the Piedmont (**peed**-mont) Plateau. Piedmont means "foot of the mountain." The Piedmont Plateau is high, flat land. It is near several mountain ranges in the eastern United States.

Major highways and railroads connect cities on the Piedmont Plateau. Many people and goods move between these cities. Airports, highways, and railroads connect these manufacturing centers with other communities in the United States.

Goods made in Thomasville and nearby communities are sold in all parts of the United States. About 25 trucking companies carry materials and goods to and from the area.

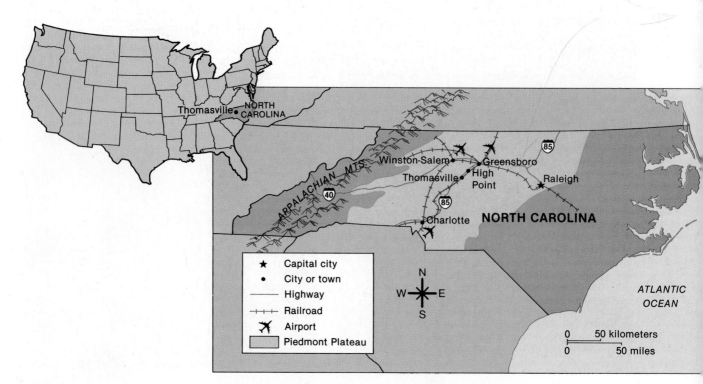

Thomasville is in a part of the United States called the Sunbelt. Thomasville has long, hot summers and short, mild winters. Plenty of rain helps flowers, plants, and trees grow well.

Not all parts of the United States have such a comfortable climate. This pleasant climate attracts people to the community. It also attracts new companies. New companies bring more jobs and more goods and services. Sunbelt cities have been growing quickly in the last 10 years. In Thomasville, there are more furniture companies today than ever before.

Great Smoky Mountain National Park, North Carolina

Section Review

Write your answers on a sheet of paper.
1. Name two natural resources used in Thomasville's industry.
2. How are the cities on the Piedmont Plateau connected?
3. Compare winter in Thomasville to winter in Pella.

2 How Thomasville Began

"The railroad is coming!"

This news gave John W. Thomas of North Carolina an idea. A good place to start a community would be along a railroad. A railroad would help a community grow. So Thomas bought land along the route of a new railroad. In 1852, he began to build a town. The town became Thomasville, North Carolina.

In the 1850's, many railroads in the United States were just starting. People like John Thomas saw how important railroads could be. Railroads would give people a way to get to new communities. Railroads would give both new and old communities a way to transport goods and materials to each other. In this way, industries would grow. The United States would grow too.

At first, Thomasville was a village. It had only a few buildings and not much industry. Two companies made shoes, and another made bricks.

The train from New Orleans, Louisiana, to Mobile, Alabama, February 1874

One early industry was started by D. S. Westmoreland. He began to make chairs in his home. By 1879, he had built a **factory,** or a building in which to manufacture his chairs. It was the first chair factory in North Carolina.

Thomasville grew slowly until the railroad was finished. Then more people came to Thomasville. New stores, banks, and hotels opened. New factories were built. The factories made shoes, doors, saddles, cabinets, and chairs. **Mills** opened too. A mill is a building with machines to make such things as flour or cloth. Mills in Thomasville began to make cotton cloth and stockings. The small town became a large town.

factory
a building where goods are manufactured

mill
a building with machines to make such things as flour or cloth

White Oak Mills, Greensboro, North Carolina, 1907

Section Review

Write your answers on a sheet of paper.
1. Describe how Thomasville was started.
2. How do railroads help a community grow?
3. Are there factories in your community or in other communities in your state? What is made in them?

3 Thomasville Today

Factories in North Carolina make more wooden furniture than factories in any other state. Some of this furniture is made in Thomasville.

More than 4,500 people work in Thomasville's furniture industry. The chart on this page shows some of the jobs they do. When furniture is made, each step must be done carefully and with skill. Study the chart to see how pieces of wood become pieces of furniture. It takes up to a year to finish all the steps.

Making table legs

Packing furniture for shipping

Many other people in the community work at jobs that help the furniture industry. One company makes mirrors. Another makes special curved parts for chairs or bedposts. Other companies make chemicals used in stains and finishes for wooden furniture. Stains add color to the wood. Finishes give furniture a smooth, polished look. They also protect it.

The pictures on this page show different kinds of work that help the furniture industry. Some companies make chair cushions. Others make knobs, handles, and hinges. These are used on cabinets and drawers.

An industry is important to a community. It provides jobs for people. It buys goods or services from other companies in the community. It pays taxes that are used to provide services in the community.

Sometimes businesses give money for special community needs. The pictures show two things a community might pay for with this money.

Ambulance rescue squad

Community concert, Grandfather's Mountain, North Carolina

An industry can help a community in other ways too. Thomasville's furniture manufacturers work closely with a state college. They help set up classes in furniture making.

Thomasville's furniture industry makes use of buildings in nearby communities. For example, the community of High Point, North Carolina, has big buildings to display furniture. Buyers from furniture stores all over the United States shop in the showrooms at High Point.

Communities in different parts of the United States make many other kinds of goods. In communities in the Northeast, factories produce many products made from chemicals. Some of these products are rayon cloth, paints, and plastics. Other factories in this area make television sets, film for cameras, and clothing.

Communities in the Central United States such as Detroit, Michigan, manufacture cars, trucks, and buses. People in other industries in this area package farmers' crops into foods for stores.

Furniture-making class, Catawba Valley Technical College, North Carolina

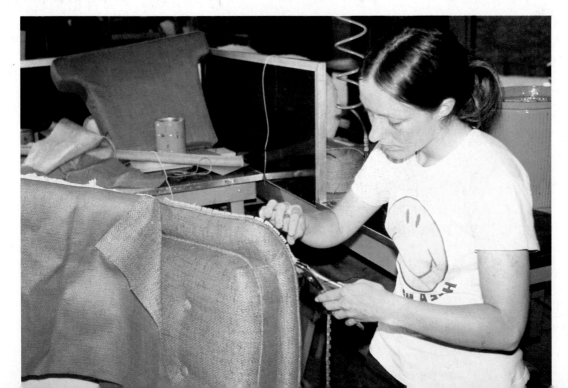

One of the biggest industries in the Southwest is turning oil into gasoline and other products. In communities in the Far West, airplanes, airplane equipment, and food products are made.

Look at the map. What natural resource do many of these areas have in common?

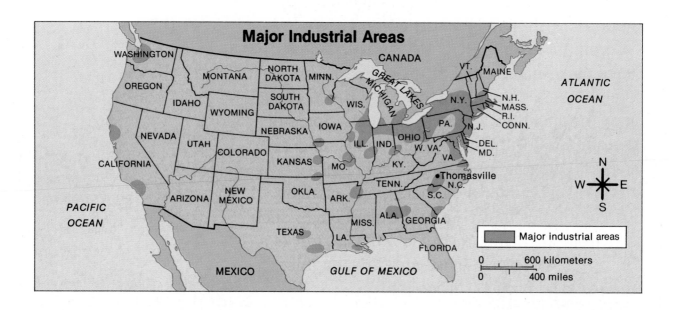

Major Industrial Areas

Section Review

Write your answers on a sheet of paper.
1. Name three jobs people do in the furniture industry.
2. Name four ways that an industry helps a community.
3. Why do you think it is important to follow directions carefully when making a piece of furniture?

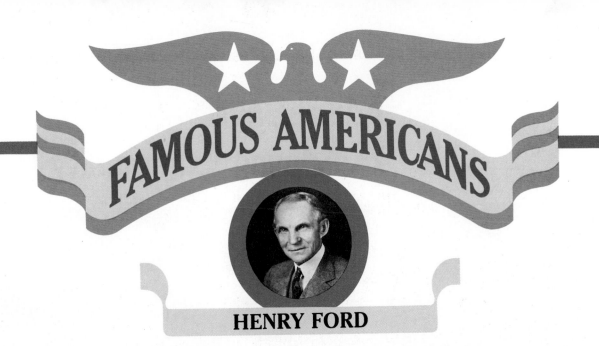

FAMOUS AMERICANS

HENRY FORD

As a boy growing up in Michigan, Henry Ford was interested in machines. When he grew up, he invented a motor car. Today, Detroit, Michigan, is an important car manufacturing city.

In the early 1900's, there were some cars on the roads, but they were all very expensive. Since Ford was very good at working with machines, he decided to use his skill to make a car that would not cost so much.

In 1903, Henry Ford started the Ford Motor Company. The first car he manufactured was the Model A. It cost $850. His second car was the Model T. In 1914, it cost only $440, a price many people could afford.

Ford built factories to make the parts his cars needed. Workers put cars together on an assembly line. In this process, workers stand in one place. The cars go by on a moving belt. As each car passes by, a worker adds a part. The worker does the same job on each car. Henry Ford used the assembly line to make more cars in less time.

Henry Ford gave people a faster way to get from place to place. He gave many people jobs in his factories, and he paid them good wages.

Henry Ford was not only good at working with machines, he was good at working with people.

9 Madisonville— A Mining Community

A coal field in Paradise, Kentucky

People in Madisonville, Kentucky, call their community "The Best Town on Earth." It is a town with many old buildings. But it also has many new buildings.

In this chapter, you will learn about the history of Madisonville. You will read about the work people do there.

At the end of this chapter, you should be able to:
○ Explain how transportation is important to the agriculture and industry of a community.
○ List the main resources of Madisonville.
○ List some of the ways people earn money in Madisonville.

1 Resources and Climate

Kentucky is in the center of the eastern part of the United States. Find Madisonville on the map. Many highways and railroads connect this community with other communities in the United States. Two big rivers, the Ohio and the Mississippi, are nearby. Freight is carried on these highways, railroads, and rivers. Madisonville also has an airport. Freight is flown to and from the airport.

The airport, highways, railroads, and rivers are important to Madisonville. Goods from Madisonville may be sent to many places by plane, truck, train, and boat. Large cities such as Chicago and St. Louis are centers for transportation. From Chicago and St. Louis, Madisonville's resources and products can be shipped all over the world.

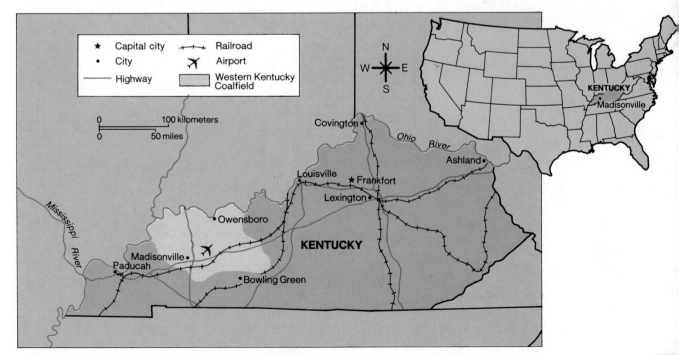

mineral
a substance found in nature that is not an animal or a plant

mining
the process of taking mineral resources from the earth

bituminous coal
soft coal

Madisonville is in the Western Kentucky Coalfield. Coal is a **mineral.** A mineral is a substance found in nature that is not an animal or a plant. To use this mineral, it must be taken out of the earth. The process of taking mineral resources out of the earth is called **mining.**

Soft coal, or **bituminous** (bih-**too**-muh-nus) **coal,** is mined in western Kentucky. This coal is burned in power plants to make energy for homes and factories.

The coal in Kentucky is mined in two ways. Some coal is found deep underground. This coal is removed from the earth by a method called deep coal mining. In the Western Kentucky Coalfield, another type of mining is used. In this area, the coal is found close to the surface. To mine this coal, layers of earth are removed. This type of mining is called strip mining.

Madisonville also has resources other than coal. The rich soil and mild, rainy climate are good for farming. Corn is the biggest crop grown around Madisonville. Much of it is used to feed the many cattle, sheep, and pigs that are raised there. Soybeans and tobacco are other important crops.

Section Review

Write your answers on a sheet of paper.
1. Name two resources found near Madisonville.
2. Describe two ways that coal is mined in Kentucky.
3. Why is good transportation important for coal mining and agriculture?

2 Madisonville's Early Days

More than 40 American Indian villages once stood where Madisonville is today. We know about them because people have found things made and used by the Indians. But not much more is known about these early Indians. They were gone before people from Europe came to explore the area.

In 1792, Kentucky became the fifteenth state in the United States. At that time, it was farther west than any other state. At the same time, James Madison was an official in the United States government. He thought that the nation would become stronger if more families moved to Kentucky. More people in the West would mean more trade on the Mississippi River.

In 1806, Hopkins County was formed. In 1807, Daniel McGrary and Solomon Silkwood each gave some of their land for a county seat. The land had many springs with good drinking water. The new community was named Madisonville, after James Madison. At first the town grew slowly.

Early settlers in Kentucky

Coal mining in the early 1900's

Madisonville remained a small town for a long time. People knew there was coal in the area. They could see the coal on hillsides where the soil had washed or fallen away. But people used only small amounts of this coal. Most of their coal was transported by riverboat from Pittsburgh, Pennsylvania.

Then, in 1870, a railroad was built to Madisonville. The new railroad was used mainly to move farm products to other parts of the country. But the trains could also move coal. Because of this transportation, a coal industry was started. People came to Madisonville on the railroad. The town and the coal industry grew rapidly.

More and more people came to Madisonville to work in the coal industry. Many other people came to provide services for the growing population. By 1940, 8,000 people lived in Madisonville. Now the population is almost three times as large as in 1940. And Madisonville is still growing.

Section Review

Write your answers on a sheet of paper.
1. How do we know about the Indians who lived around Madisonville?
2. Who was Madisonville named after?
3. What two things helped the city grow more quickly?

3 Madisonville Today

More people in Madisonville today work in the mining industry than in any other industry. Many of them learn how to do their jobs at a special training school. People go to this school after finishing high school. An artificial mine was built at the training school to help teach students about mining. The "mine" is an underground room that is about the same size as part of a real coal mine. Students learn how to dig for coal and use mine equipment safely.

The community college in Madisonville works with the training school to get people ready for jobs in the coal industry. Students learn to be inspectors, managers, equipment salespeople, and other kinds of workers. They also learn how to **reclaim** land. Reclaiming land means making it beautiful or useful again. If the ground is left bare after strip mining, nothing can grow there. More soil can be washed away by rain. To reclaim the land, the soil is replaced, and grasses or other crops are planted. This keeps the soil in place.

reclaim
to make useful again

*(left) Land used for strip mining
(right) Strip mining land that has been reclaimed*

Other industries have started in Madisonville because of coal mining. Factories make many kinds of equipment, especially mining equipment. Many people work in these factories. Others work for the railroads that carry coal and other goods to other cities.

Some of the other products manufactured in Madisonville are jet engine parts, tires, laundry equipment, and dairy products. Transportation is important for all these industries. Supplies for making these products must be brought to the factories. And the products are sold in places far from Madisonville.

Madisonville also has a large medical center and school. People are trained to be nurses and medical secretaries. They learn to work with doctors in the operating room. They learn to work in laboratories and do many other jobs.

Worker in an electrical plant, Madisonville

Madisonville offers its citizens many ways to enjoy themselves. There are parks in the area where people can sail, fish, hike, picnic, or camp. Some people belong to a group that puts on plays for the community. Many take part in sports activities. Madisonville also has many restaurants and movie theaters.

All of these things make the people of Madisonville proud of their community. They really believe it is the best town on earth.

Section Review

Write your answers on a sheet of paper.
1. What is the main industry in Madisonville?
2. What does "reclaiming land" mean?
3. How has coal mining helped other industries grow in Madisonville?

CHAPTER 10

Washington, D.C.— A Government Community

Our country's government is located in Washington, D.C. This community is our nation's capital.

In this chapter, you will learn about Washington, D.C. You will learn how the community began and some of the work that goes on there today.

At the end of this chapter, you should be able to:

○ Describe where Washington, D.C., is located.

○ Explain why the capital city was so carefully planned.

○ Name some jobs people do in Washington, D.C.

● Read a timetable.

1 A New City

In 1776, the government of our country was started. At that time, communities such as Boston, New York, and Philadelphia were already cities. But Washington, D.C., was not yet a city. It was not even a small town. It was only forests and fields.

The new government was first located in Philadelphia. Next it was moved to Baltimore and then to several other cities. In 1783, government leaders decided the government should be in one city all the time. But no one could agree on where the capital city should be. People from different cities all thought that their city should be made the capital.

In 1790, government leaders came up with a plan. They decided to build a new city to be the nation's capital.

Near the Potomac River, before Washington, D.C., was built

In 1790, our country had 13 states. The states agreed to build the new city between Virginia and Maryland. President George Washington knew this part of the country well. He was asked to choose the best place for the new capital. In 1791, he picked a spot along the Potomac (puh-**toe**-mik) River.

Look at the map. It shows the young United States. It also shows the spot chosen for the new capital city. People would be able to reach the capital by traveling along the Potomac River.

The place chosen for Washington, D.C., was not part of any state. It was a **district,** or an area set aside for a special purpose. The district was named Columbia. Washington, D.C., means Washington, District of Columbia.

Most cities were once small villages. In a village, footpaths wound from place to place. As

district

an area set aside for a special purpose

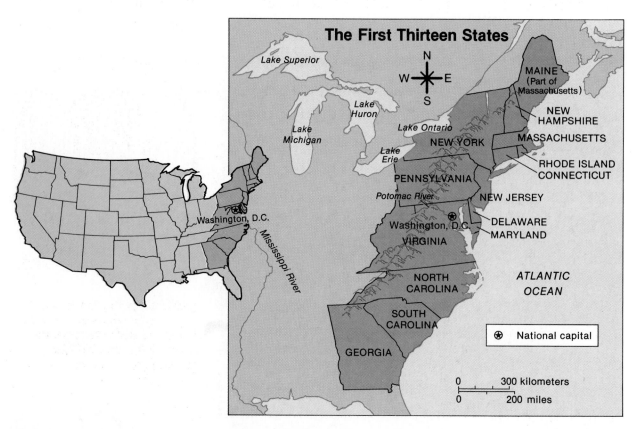

The First Thirteen States

Lake Superior

Lake Huron

Lake Michigan

Lake Ontario

Lake Erie

MAINE (Part of Massachusetts)

NEW HAMPSHIRE

NEW YORK

MASSACHUSETTS

RHODE ISLAND

CONNECTICUT

PENNSYLVANIA

NEW JERSEY

Potomac River

DELAWARE

Washington, D.C.

MARYLAND

VIRGINIA

ATLANTIC OCEAN

NORTH CAROLINA

SOUTH CAROLINA

GEORGIA

Washington, D.C.

Mississippi River

⊛ National capital

0   300 kilometers
0   200 miles

a village grew, footpaths became city streets. This is why many older cities have narrow streets. People did not plan the city's growth. Little space was left for parks or wide streets.

George Washington did not want the capital city to grow this way. He wanted a beautiful, well-planned city. He asked a French engineer named Pierre L'Enfant (**pyair** lahn-**fahn**) to design the new capital. L'Enfant planned where streets, parks, and buildings would go.

Work on the new capital city began in 1791. First land had to be carefully measured. Much of this work was done by a **surveyor** named Benjamin Banneker. The building of the new capital city continued until the early 1800's.

In 1800, the government moved into the new capital city. Washington, D.C., became the home of the government for all of the United States. We call this kind of government the **federal government.**

surveyor
a person who carefully measures land

federal government
the government of all the states together

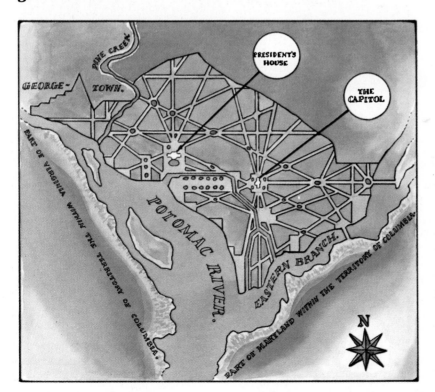

(left) L'Enfant's plan for the capital city   (above) Portrait of Benjamin Banneker from the early 1800's, with the old spelling of his name

Since 1800, our country has grown to 50 states. As the country has grown, so has the government. More and more people are needed to make the government work. As more people came to Washington, D.C., to work for the government, the city grew.

Look at the pictures on this page. One picture shows an early view of the city. The other pictures show how the capital had grown by 1900 and how it looks today.

Washington, D.C., 1824

Washington, D.C., 1900

Washington, D.C., today

Section Review

Write your answers on a sheet of paper.
1. Explain how the capital city of the United States was chosen.
2. How did Pierre L'Enfant help make a new capital city for the United States?
3. How has Washington, D.C., grown since 1800?

2 A Government City

People do many different jobs in Washington, D.C. Perhaps the best-known job is that of the President of the United States. The President's duty is to make sure the laws of the land are carried out.

Some women and men in Washington, D.C., work as lawmakers. They **represent** the people of their own state or area. "To represent" means "to speak or act for a person or a group of people."

In very small communities, all the people can vote on each law. In a large country such as the United States, however, lawmakers vote on each law. People elect lawmakers called senators and representatives to represent them. The nation's laws are made by these elected representatives.

Some government workers are chosen, not elected. Judges in the Supreme Court, for example, are chosen by the President. Their job is to decide whether or not the laws of the land have been broken.

represent
to speak or act
for a person or a
group of people

*Meeting of the Senate and
House of Representatives*

Most government workers are neither elected nor chosen. They are hired to do jobs that keep the government running. Some of these workers are postal carriers, secretaries, scientists, and pages. Pages are young people who carry messages and run errands for representatives.

The map shows some of the federal buildings in the capital. Find the White House, where the President and the President's family live. Find the Capitol Building, where the laws of the land are made. Find the Department of Agriculture. People work there to help the farmers of the United States. Find the Bureau of Engraving and Printing. Workers there print the bills we use as money.

Over the years, many leaders have worked in our government. Some buildings in the capital honor past government leaders.

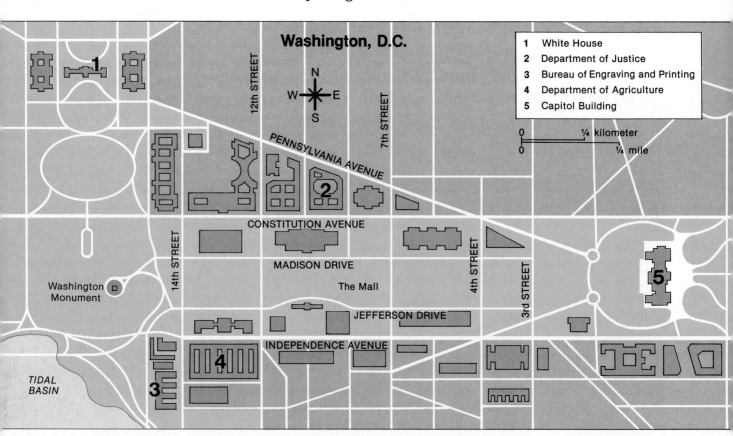

Washington, D.C.

1	White House
2	Department of Justice
3	Bureau of Engraving and Printing
4	Department of Agriculture
5	Capitol Building

0   ¼ kilometer
0   ¼ mile

PENNSYLVANIA AVENUE
12th STREET
7th STREET
CONSTITUTION AVENUE
14th STREET
4th STREET
3rd STREET
MADISON DRIVE
The Mall
JEFFERSON DRIVE
INDEPENDENCE AVENUE
Washington Monument
TIDAL BASIN

The Jefferson Memorial was built for the nation's third President, Thomas Jefferson. A **memorial** is something built or done as a reminder of a person or event. A memorial can be a building, statue, book, holiday, or any other reminder.

The Lincoln Memorial was built to remember Abraham Lincoln. He was our nation's sixteenth President. Inside the memorial is a famous statue of Lincoln.

A **monument** is also something that helps us to remember a person or event. A monument is usually a building of some kind. The Washington Monument honors George Washington, our first President. Today visitors can travel to the top of this monument in an elevator. From the top, visitors can clearly see the city Pierre L'Enfant designed so many years ago.

memorial
something built or done to help remember a person or event

monument
something built to honor a person or event

(left) Jefferson Memorial
(middle) Lincoln Memorial
(right) Washington Monument

Today over a million people live in the nation's capital and its suburbs. Many of them work for the federal government. Thousands of people visit the city every day. They come from around the world. They come from every state. Many people visit the capital to look at the buildings and monuments. Some Americans come to talk to their senators and representatives. They want to let their government know their wants and needs.

Many people visit Washington, D.C., in the spring when the cherry trees bloom.

Section Review

Write your answers on a sheet of paper.
1. What are some of the different kinds of jobs people do for the federal government?
2. Why do people elect representatives?
3. What is a memorial?
4. What memorials or monuments have you seen or heard of? What people or events did these memorials or monuments honor?

Reading a Timetable

Have you ever taken a trip? How did you know what time to be at the airport or station? One way to find out is to check a **timetable.** A table is a chart that lists different facts. What kinds of facts are listed in a timetable?

Look at the timetable for a bus trip from Washington, D.C., to New York City. The table shows that buses leave at different times during the week and on weekends. To find out when a bus leaves Washington, D.C., look in the "Leave" column. Which column tells when buses arrive in New York City? Which side of the timetable tells about weekend buses?

timetable

a chart that tells when buses, trains, or planes arrive or leave

Bus Schedule Washington, D.C., to New York City			
Mondays to Fridays		Weekends	
Leave Washington	Arrive New York	Leave Washington	Arrive New York
6:00 A. M.	11:00 A. M.	7:00 A. M.	NOON
6:30 A. M.	11:30 A. M.	8:00 A. M.	1:00 P. M.
7:00 A. M.	NOON	9:00 A. M.	2:00 P. M.
7:30 A. M.	12:30 P. M.	10:30 A. M.	3:30 P. M.
8:00 A. M.	1:00 P. M.	NOON	5:00 P. M.
9:00 A. M.	2:00 P. M.	1:30 P. M.	6:30 P. M.
10:00 A. M.	3:00 P. M.	3:00 P. M.	8:00 P. M.
11:00 A. M.	4:00 P. M.	4:30 P. M.	9:30 P. M.
NOON	5:00 P. M.	6:00 P. M.	11:00 P. M.
1:00 P. M.	6:00 P. M.		
2:00 P. M.	7:00 P. M.		
3:00 P. M.	8:00 P. M.		
4:00 P. M.	9:00 P. M.		
5:00 P. M.	10:00 P. M.		

═══ Practice Your Skills ═══

1. When does the earliest bus from Washington, D.C., arrive in New York City?
2. What time does the last bus leave for New York City on Sundays?
3. About how long is a bus trip between Washington, D.C., and New York City?

11 Honolulu— A Tourist Community

Waikiki Beach, Honolulu, Hawaii

"Aloha" (uh-**loe**-ha), or "welcome," to beautiful Honolulu (hahn-uh-**loo**-loo). Millions of people visit Honolulu each year. They come to enjoy the sunny weather and beautiful scenery.

In this chapter, you will learn about some of the places of interest in Honolulu. You will learn about some of the people who live there and the jobs they do. You will also learn about the landforms in this part of our country.

At the end of this chapter, you should be able to:
○ Describe what a volcano is.
● Read a landforms map.
○ Explain how Honolulu's location helped the city to grow.
○ Name ways people in Honolulu earn money.

1 An Island State

Honolulu is the capital of the state of Hawaii (huh-**wah**-ee). It is also the largest city in the state. Most of the people living in Hawaii live in Honolulu.

Hawaii is made up of many islands. Eight of Hawaii's islands are large islands. These large islands are Hawaii, Maui (**mou**-ee), Oahu (uh-**wah**-hoo), Kauai (kuh-**wah**-ee), Molokai (moe-luh-**kie**), Lanai (lah-**nah**-ee), Niihau (**nee**-hou), and Kahoolawe (kah-hoo-**lah**-weh). Some of the islands have nicknames. Hawaii is called Big Island. Kauai is called Garden Island. Lanai is called Pineapple Island because of the pineapples grown there.

Hawaii lies near the middle of the Pacific Ocean. Since 1778, when the Hawaiian Islands were first visited by Europeans, they have been the resting point for people crossing this huge body of water. Look at the map. On which island is Honolulu? Which island is the largest?

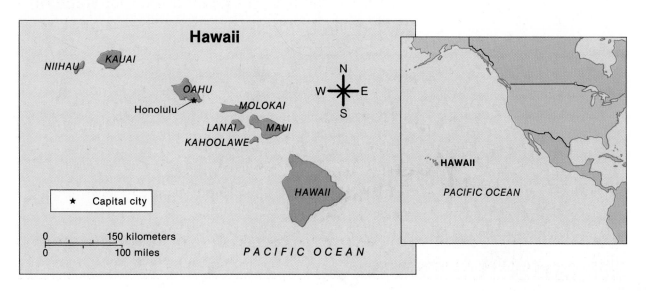

volcano
a mountain with an opening through which gas and rock can escape

erupt
to explode

lava
melted rock

Some scientists believe that the islands of Hawaii were formed millions of years ago by **volcanoes.** A volcano is a mountain with an opening at the top. This opening goes down deep inside the earth to where temperatures are hot enough to melt rock. Steam and melted rock sometimes explode, or **erupt,** from volcanoes. The melted rock, or **lava,** flows down the sides of the mountain and onto the land around it. The lava cools and becomes hard, rocky land. The mountain may grow taller and bigger as more and more lava cools on its top and sides.

Some volcanoes are at the bottom of the sea. The Hawaiian Islands may be the tops of such volcanoes. And these islands are still growing! In some parts of Hawaii, volcanoes still erupt. Lava from these volcanoes flows into the sea. Then the lava cools on the ocean floor. As more and more lava flows into the ocean and cools, new land is formed.

A volcano erupting, Hawaii

On the island of Oahu, in Hawaii

The Hawaiian Islands stretch about 2,444 kilometers (1,519 miles) across the Pacific Ocean. Hawaii is the southernmost part of the United States. Hawaii's climate is sunny and warm. The temperature is nearly the same during the summer and winter months. People from all over the world come to Hawaii to enjoy its mild weather and beautiful beaches.

Section Review

Write your answers on a sheet of paper.
1. What is a volcano?
2. How is the land of Hawaii still growing?
3. Why do you think so many people visit Hawaii each year?

Reading a Landforms Map

landforms map

a map that uses color to show the height and form of the land

You already know that a cutaway diagram can show the height and form of the land. A **landforms map** can also show the height and form of the land. On a landforms map, color is used to show what the land is like.

Below is a cutaway diagram of the Hawaiian island of Oahu. Notice that the mountains are colored red. What color are the lowlands? the plateaus? Next to the diagram is a landforms map of the island. Study the map key. Red is also used on the landforms map to show mountains. What does green stand for? What color is used to show plateaus on the landforms map?

A landforms map of the whole United States is on the next page. How many different colors are used on this map? What type of landform does each color stand for? You can see that bodies of water are also shown on a landforms map. What rivers can you find on the map? What other bodies of water can you find?

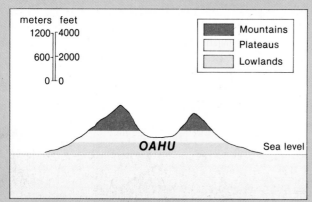

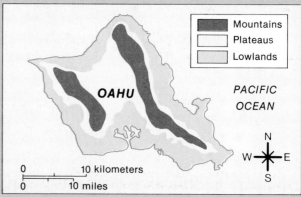

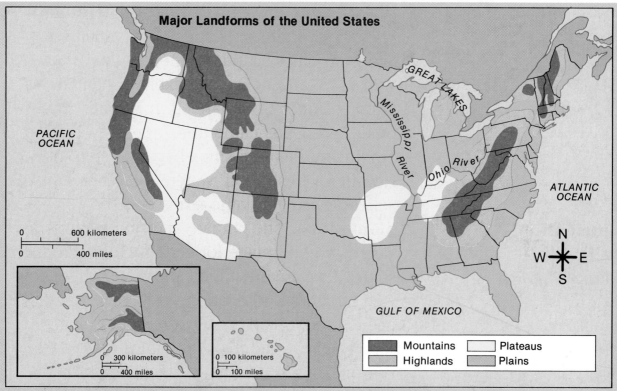

Major Landforms of the United States

PACIFIC OCEAN

GREAT LAKES

Mississippi River

Ohio River

ATLANTIC OCEAN

0   600 kilometers
0   400 miles

GULF OF MEXICO

N W E S

0   300 kilometers
0   400 miles

0   100 kilometers
0   100 miles

Mountains   Plateaus
Highlands   Plains

Practice Your Skills

1. What color is used to show plains on the United States map? What color is used to show highlands?
2. What is the highest kind of landform in the central United States? What is the highest kind of landform in the western United States?
3. In what kind of landform area are the Great Lakes found?
4. Are there more plateaus in the eastern states or western states?

2 Past and Present

The first people to discover the Hawaiian Islands were Polynesians (pahl-uh-**nee**-zhunz). They came to these islands about 2,000 years ago from other islands in the Pacific.

In 1778, an English sea explorer named Captain James Cook landed in Hawaii. Soon other Europeans came to explore Hawaii. Trading and fishing ships began to stop in Hawaii for fresh food, water, and other supplies.

People planted large farms called **plantations.** The climate and rich land made Hawaii a good place for certain crops. Products such as sugarcane, pineapple, and coffee grow well in Hawaii. Plantations grew bigger and needed more workers. People from China, Japan, Korea, and the Philippines came to Hawaii to work on the plantations.

Everyone who came to Hawaii traveled by ship. Most ships landed in a bay on one of the large islands. A community began to grow on this bay. It was named Honolulu, which is the Hawaiian word for "sheltered bay."

plantation

a large farm where one crop is grown

Captain James Cook lands in Hawaii, 1778

Pineapples are big business in Hawaii.

Today Honolulu has grown into a busy place. In the harbor, ships are loaded with sugarcane and pineapples. Manufacturers make clothing, cement, and many other products. There are large factories where some of Hawaii's food products are put into cans. These factories are called **canneries.** Fishing is another important industry in Hawaii.

Honolulu's airport is always busy. About 900 planes take off and land in Honolulu every day!

One of the biggest businesses in Honolulu is **tourism.** Tourism is the business of supplying services to visitors. Large numbers of people living in Honolulu earn money by working for the tourist industry. Many Hawaiians have jobs in hotels, restaurants, or gift shops. These places supply things that tourists want or need.

cannery
a factory where food products are put into cans

tourism
the business of supplying services to visitors

157

Tourists visit Honolulu to enjoy the good weather and the beautiful scenery. One of the best-known sights is Diamond Head. Diamond Head is a volcano that no longer erupts. It is located at the southeastern tip of Oahu. Tourists also spend time at Waikiki (**wie**-kee-kee) Beach. Many hotels and restaurants are near this beach area. People visit Aloha Tower to see the view of Honolulu's harbor. Many people go to Kapiolani (kahp-ee-oe-**lah**-ni) Park to listen to concerts and visit the zoo.

Tourists also come to Hawaii to enjoy the Hawaiian culture. A visitor is often welcomed with a lei (**lay**-ee), or chain of flowers, placed around the neck.

Tourists might go to a Hawaiian feast called a luau (**loo**-ow). At a luau, people eat traditional Hawaiian foods. Women at a luau often wear muumuus (**moo**-mooz), which are loose-fitting, floor-length dresses. Men wear colorful shirts called aloha shirts. Visitors might watch a special Hawaiian dance called the hula (**hoo**-luh).

Hawaiians doing the hula

More than 3 million tourists visit Honolulu each year. Honolulu is a tourist community. This means that much of the business of the community depends on tourists.

There are many other tourist communities in the United States. Williamsburg, Virginia, is a popular place for tourists. In this community, visitors see how people lived in the 1700's. Camden, Maine, is an old fishing village that many tourists visit. What are some tourist places you have seen? Maybe some day you will visit Honolulu. What are some of the things you would like to do while you are there?

(left) Williamsburg, Virginia
(middle) Camden, Maine
(right) Honolulu, Hawaii

Section Review

Write your answers on a sheet of paper.
1. Who discovered the Hawaiian Islands?
2. Explain how the community of Honolulu began.
3. What is a luau?
4. Compare your community with a tourist community. How are they the same? How are they different?

Work Songs

"I've got a mule, her name is Sal,
Fifteen miles on the Erie Canal!"

A canal is a human-made waterway. In the 1800's, the Erie Canal helped connect the American East with the West. Mules pulled barges filled with goods through the canal. The Erie Canal was 580 kilometers (360 miles) long, but the barges could move only as fast as the mules could walk. Barge workers sang this song to make the slow trip seem faster:

"We've hauled some barges in our day.
Filled with lumber, coal and hay,
And every inch of the way we know
From Albany to Buffalo."

People have always enjoyed singing while they work. Their songs were often about the kind of work they were doing. This is a song that railroad workers sang:

"Here she comes, look at her roll,
There she goes, eating that coal.

Watch her fly, look at her sail.
Let her by, it's the Fireball Mail!"

Building the railroads across the United States was hard work. Singing helped the workers forget the heat of the sun and the aches in their backs. Singing also helped them feel better when they were lonely after the day's work was done.

"I'm a'walkin' down the track,
I got tears in my eyes,
Tryin' to read a letter from my home."

Important work was also done in people's homes. Pioneers did not have stores nearby where they could buy goods. People had to grow their

America

own food and sew their own clothes. Women used spinning wheels to make thread for sewing. Spinning wheels twisted clumps of cotton or wool into thread. Foot pedals made the wheels turn. Singing helped the women keep a steady rhythm as they pumped the pedals. That was the purpose of this song, whose words have no meaning:

"Sa-ra-spon-da, Sa-ra-spon-da, Sa-ra-spon-da, Ret-set-set!"

UNIT REVIEW

Word Work

Write the sentences below on a sheet of paper. Fill in the blanks with the correct words from the list.

reclaim   manufacturing   represent   agriculture

1. If you speak for a group, you ____ it.
2. The business of farming is called ____.
3. Producing goods by machine is called ____.
4. To make old mining land beautiful or useful again, people have to ____ it.

Knowing the Facts

Write your answers on a sheet of paper.
1. What natural resources does a farm community need?
2. How can an industry help a community?
3. Name two ways that leaders of the past are honored in Washington, D.C.
4. How does tourism help a community?

Using What You Know

Choose one of the following activities to do. Follow the instructions given here.
1. Make a picture graph to show how many books you read in each week of a month.
2. Make a travel poster showing what people can see and do if they visit one of the communities described in this unit.

Skills Practice

Use the following map to answer the questions below. Write your answers on a sheet of paper.

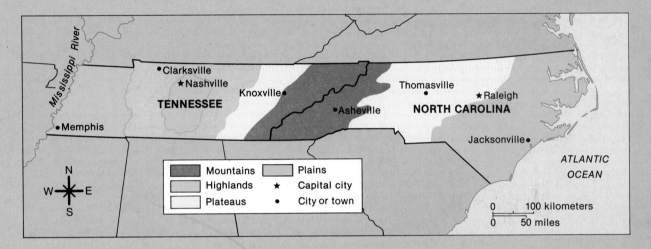

1. What color shows plateaus? plains? What part of the map tells what the colors mean?
2. In what kind of landform area is Thomasville, North Carolina? Jacksonville? Asheville?
3. Are there more highlands in North Carolina or in Tennessee?
4. Is the land along the Mississippi River highland or lowland?

Your Community

Every community has special reasons to be proud. What are some reasons to be proud of your community? Does your community have a special festival? If not, what kind of festival could your community hold to honor an event of the past?

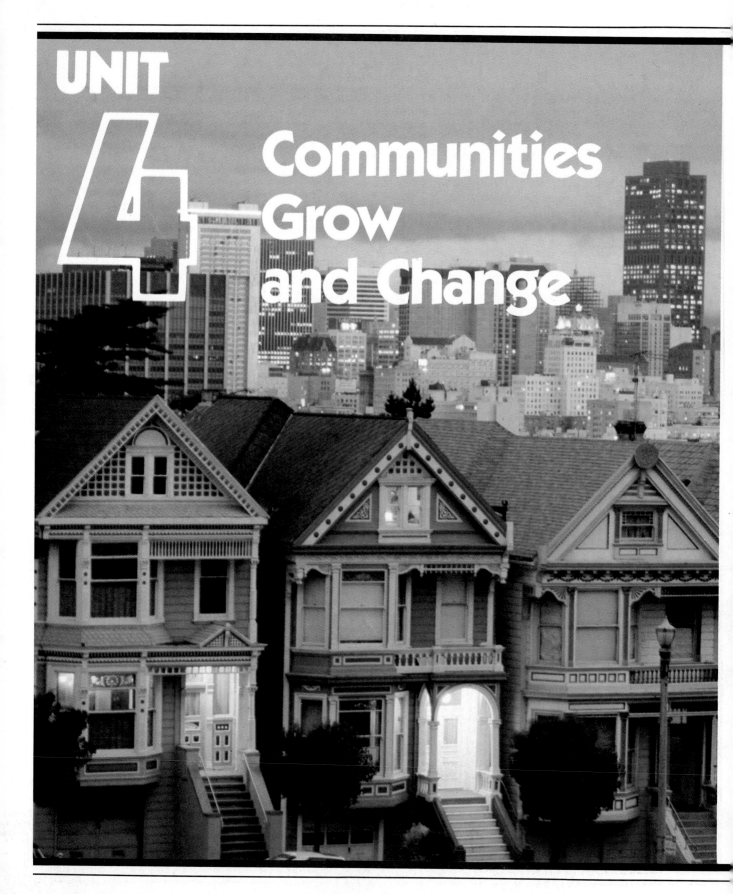

UNIT 4

Communities Grow and Change

Communities grow and change for different reasons. When people move in or out of a community, the community changes. Sometimes new industries bring changes to a community.

Sometimes growing causes problems. If a community grows too quickly, its services may not be able to keep up with its needs.

In this unit, you will read about three communities and how they have grown and changed.

CHAPTER **12** San Francisco— A City Reaches Out

San Francisco, 1838

In 1769, Spanish explorers discovered a large bay on the west coast of North America. A new settlement was soon started on the bay. It was called Yerba Buena (**yehr**-buh **bway**-nuh) and later San Francisco. Today San Francisco is a big city.

At the end of this chapter, you should be able to:

○ Explain why San Francisco Bay is important to the communities around it.

○ Describe events that helped San Francisco grow.

○ Explain how San Francisco has solved some of its problems.

● Read a flow chart.

1 The Bay Area

Look at the map on this page and find San Francisco. San Francisco, California, is on a piece of land almost entirely surrounded by water. The city is on a peninsula.

Three bodies of water surround San Francisco. West of San Francisco is the Pacific Ocean. To the east of the city is San Francisco Bay. A body of water called a **channel** connects the ocean to the bay. This channel is called the Golden Gate. The Golden Gate Bridge crosses it.

The bay is 80 kilometers (50 miles) long and in some places 19 kilometers (12 miles) wide. A long bridge connects San Francisco to the city of Oakland and other communities across the bay. This bridge is called the San Francisco–Oakland Bay Bridge.

channel
a body of water that connects two other bodies of water

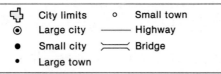

⊕ City limits	○ Small town
◉ Large city	—— Highway
● Small city	⊐⊏ Bridge
• Large town	

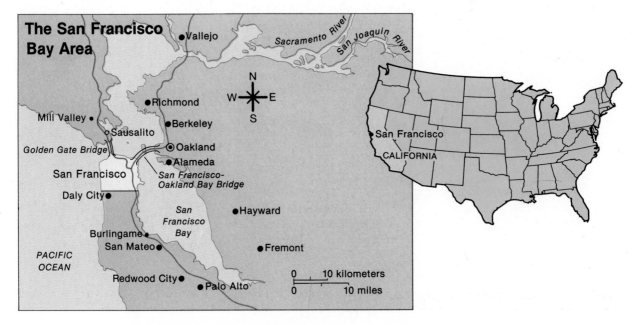

The San Francisco Bay Area

Vallejo
Sacramento River
San Joaquin River

Richmond
Mill Valley
Berkeley
Sausalito
Golden Gate Bridge
Oakland
Alameda
San Francisco
San Francisco–Oakland Bay Bridge
Daly City
San Francisco Bay
Hayward
Burlingame
San Mateo
Fremont
PACIFIC OCEAN
Redwood City
Palo Alto

0   10 kilometers
0   10 miles

San Francisco
CALIFORNIA

metropolitan area
a city and the communities around it

A city and the communities around it make up a **metropolitan area.** San Francisco and many other communities around San Francisco Bay make up the San Francisco metropolitan area. The bay is the center of a big shipping industry. On the bay, ships can dock at any one of eight ports. Goods from all over the world are unloaded at these ports. These goods are sold in San Francisco and in other parts of the United States. Ships loaded in San Francisco Bay also carry goods to foreign nations.

Ferryboats once carried people to work in the city. Now people use the bridges to travel back and forth across the bay. Sightseeing boats still sail around the bay. Guides on these boats tell people about the city's history.

There are many places where ships can dock on San Francisco Bay.

Farmland near the Sacramento and San Joaquin rivers, California

Two rivers are important to the bay and its communities. They are the Sacramento (sack-ruh-**men**-toe) and the San Joaquin (sahn wah-**keen**). Find these rivers on the map on page 167. These rivers meet before they flow into the bay. The land near this meeting place has rich soil that is good for farming.

The rivers provide water for the crops that grow nearby. The rivers are also a means of transportation. Oceangoing ships can sail up the San Joaquin to Stockton, where they are loaded with farm products. From Stockton, they sail down river to the ocean and carry the farm products to faraway markets.

Section Review

Write your answers on a sheet of paper.
1. Name three bodies of water near San Francisco.
2. Explain why rivers are important to the Bay Area.
3. Why do you think a large metropolitan area grew around San Francisco Bay?

169

2 How San Francisco Grew

In 1776, the Spanish built a fort called the Presidio (prih-**sid**-ee-oe) in San Francisco. In the same year, Spanish priests set up a **mission** nearby. At the mission, the priests taught their religion to the American Indians in the area.

Other European settlers came to live near the Presidio and the mission. By 1848, San Francisco had about 800 people. That year, gold was discovered in the hills east of town.

Many people rushed to California to look for gold. They stopped at San Francisco for supplies. The gold rush changed San Francisco tremendously. By 1849, the community had 35,000 people. Small businesses sold goods such as food, tools, and clothing needed by the newcomers. One man, Levi Strauss, made pants from canvas cloth. Today these pants are called blue jeans.

mission

a community set up by a religious group

Montgomery Street, San Francisco, 1852

After the gold rush, San Francisco kept growing. In the 1860's, a railroad was built, starting in California. By 1869, it met and connected with a railroad that was built from the East. The railroad brought many more people to live in San Francisco.

By 1906, almost 350,000 people lived in San Francisco. That year there was a sudden shaking or trembling of the earth, called an **earthquake.** Fires broke out and soon spread. Some burned for three days. Much of the city was destroyed, and about 700 people were missing or killed.

But the earthquake did not stop the city from growing. Homes, stores, banks, and offices were rebuilt. New and stronger buildings went up quickly. Soon the city was better than new.

earthquake
sudden shaking or trembling of the earth

San Francisco after the earthquake, 1906

Section Review

Write your answers on a sheet of paper.
1. Why did people go to San Francisco in 1848?
2. How did the railroad help the city grow?
3. Why did San Francisco change after 1906?
4. As more people move to a community, what kinds of changes might take place?

3 Growing Pains

After the earthquake of 1906, San Francisco grew very quickly. When a person grows quickly, he or she can be said to have "growing pains." A city can have growing pains too.

One problem for San Francisco was space. There was not enough land for all the people who wanted to live there. Soon new communities grew up along the bay and a metropolitan area developed.

Transportation was a problem too. People living across the bay needed a fast way to get to the city to work or to shop. In the 1930's, the San Francisco–Oakland Bay Bridge and the Golden Gate Bridge were built. Now people could drive across the bay to the city.

By the 1960's, traffic on the bridges was a problem. In 1974, San Francisco opened a new railway system called <u>B</u>ay <u>A</u>rea <u>R</u>apid <u>T</u>ransit or BART. The map below shows BART routes.

BART links communities around the bay with San Francisco. Its trains travel under the bay

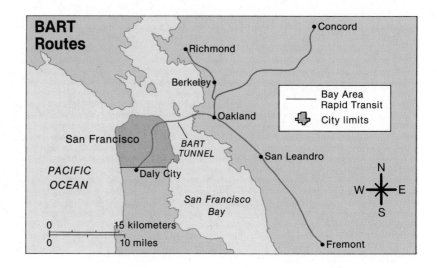

through a tunnel. BART is one way San Francisco has solved one of its problems.

Another problem for San Francisco was dirty water, or **water pollution,** in the bay. Industries dumped chemicals and waste materials into the water. These things are harmful to fish—and to people.

In the 1960's, citizens began to form groups to make some changes. They wanted to have laws passed to protect San Francisco's natural resources. Citizen groups were able to get laws passed to stop the dumping. Thousands of acres of land were set aside as parks and wildlife areas. The preservation and protection of natural resources is called **conservation.** Conservation is one way San Francisco has begun to solve one of its problems.

water pollution
dirtying of water by chemicals and waste materials

conservation
the preservation and protection of natural resources

Learning about a wildlife area near the Golden Gate

(left) A restored public square in San Francisco   (right) Restored houses on Alamo Square, San Francisco

restore

to rebuild buildings to look the way they did long ago

Another problem San Francisco faced was age. As buildings and neighborhoods grow older, they sometimes get run down. People begin to move away. Sometimes whole blocks of buildings are left empty. This happened in San Francisco.

Parts of the city needed rebuilding. The government of San Francisco **restored** many of the old buildings. They were rebuilt to look the way they did long ago. One area of old warehouses has become a big shopping and restaurant center. In other neighborhoods, beautiful old homes have been restored.

There are many beautiful neighborhoods in San Francisco today. There are also nearly 100 neighborhood groups that work hard to keep their part of the city clean and pretty. These groups also work to get good services for their part of the community. Citizens working together can help a city solve its problems.

174

The communities in the San Francisco metropolitan area have been able to solve some of their problems too. One community, Richmond, had many old, unused shipyards along its waterfront. The area was ugly and dangerous. The people of Richmond have started a project to rebuild the waterfront. New shops, offices, apartments, and parks are being built. Modern shipyards and docks are being built too.

BART has also helped Richmond. On workdays, people can travel quickly from Richmond to San Francisco. On weekends, they can easily travel to San Francisco to visit friends or see the sights.

Riding a cable car

One thing visitors in San Francisco like to do is ride the cable cars. These cars go up and down the city's steep hills. San Francisco is built on 42 hills. The city has used cable cars for more than 100 years.

The people of San Francisco are proud of their community's history. They are also proud of the work that has been done to make San Francisco a community of growth and change.

Section Review

Write your answers on a sheet of paper.
1. Name three ways people get from place to place in the bay area.
2. Why did people want to protect the bay?
3. How is San Francisco both a new and an old city?

flow chart
a chart that uses arrows to show the order in which things happen

Cleaning up water pollution is not a simple task. It takes many steps.

A clear way to show the order in which things happen is to make a **flow chart.** Look at the flow chart on this page. Arrows are used to show the order in which things happen.

The first box tells how water pollution in San Francisco Bay began. The arrow points to the next step. When the water became dirty, it became unhealthy for fish and people. Follow the arrows to the end of the chart to learn what steps the people of San Francisco took to stop water pollution.

Cleaning Up Water Pollution in San Francisco Bay

Industries dumped chemicals into San Francisco Bay. →	Fish and people were harmed. →	People formed conservation groups to make changes. ↓
		Some people removed some chemicals from the bay. ↓
The waters of the bay became healthier for fish and for people. ←	Industries stopped dumping chemicals into the bay because dumping was now against the law. ←	Others made laws to stop more dumping.

Practice Your Skills

1. What was the first step after fish and people were harmed?
2. What step came next?
3. What step shows why industries stopped dumping chemicals into the bay?
4. What happened when the dumping stopped?

FAMOUS AMERICANS

FREDERICK LAW OLMSTED

In the 1850's, most of the United States was wilderness. But Frederick Law Olmsted looked ahead and saw a different United States. He saw a time when cities would grow. He thought that farming and industry would take up more and more of the wilderness. He realized that one day, if Americans were not careful to preserve the land, there would be no more wilderness.

When he was in his forties, Olmsted camped in Yosemite (yoe-**sem**-uh-tee) Valley, California. He marveled at the huge sequoia (sih-**kwoi**-uh) trees.

In the middle of this wild valley, Olmsted met a settler. The settler told Olmsted that he planned to cut down the trees and make a ranch. But Olmsted believed that the natural beauty of Yosemite should be kept for everyone to see. Olmsted later asked Congress to make Yosemite Valley a national park. It became a national park in 1890.

At a time when New York City was mostly woods, Olmsted designed Central Park. Olmsted also designed the entire park system in Boston. It made him happy to think that city people would be able to walk along pleasant paths, smell flowers, and hear birds sing.

Frederick Law Olmsted saw the future clearly. His ideas have helped us enjoy the natural beauty of our land today.

13 Seminole— A Suburban Community

Seminole (**sem**-uh-nole), Florida, is a suburban area near the city of St. Petersburg. Many people travel from Seminole into St. Petersburg to work or shop. Many senior citizens have moved to Seminole to live. In this chapter, you will learn how Seminole changed from a small farm community into a suburban community.

At the end of this chapter, you should be able to:
○ Describe the bodies of water near Seminole.
○ Describe how the community of Seminole began.
○ Give examples of how senior citizens have improved Seminole.

1 Community on a Peninsula

The community of Seminole is in the state of Florida. Look at the map. Water surrounds almost all of Florida. Much of the state is a peninsula. Some peninsulas are large. Some peninsulas are small. The peninsula of Florida is very large compared to the peninsula of San Francisco.

Find Seminole on the map. It is near the Gulf of Mexico. A **gulf** is a large body of water with land almost all the way around it. The climate around the Gulf of Mexico is warm. Most days are sunny, and enough rain falls so that plants grow well.

gulf
a large body of water with land almost all the way around it

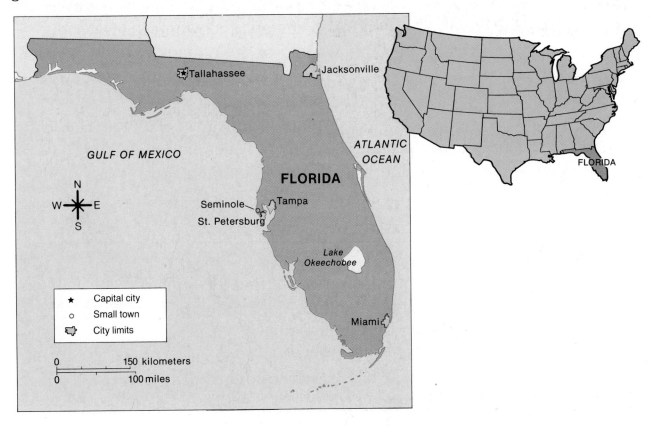

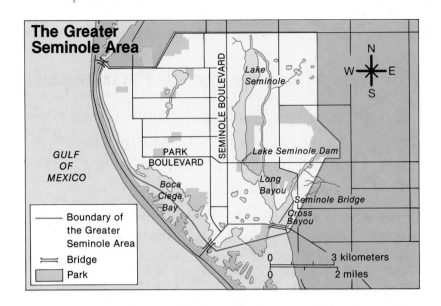

The Greater Seminole Area

N
W — E
S

GULF
OF
MEXICO

SEMINOLE BOULEVARD

Lake
Seminole

PARK
BOULEVARD

Lake Seminole Dam

Boca
Ciega
Bay

Long
Bayou

Seminole Bridge

Cross
Bayou

——— Boundary of
the Greater
Seminole Area
⊨ Bridge
Park

0   3 kilometers
0   2 miles

bayou
a stream of slow-moving water that flows into or out of another body of water such as a river or bay

lake
a body of water surrounded by land

The map on this page shows Seminole and the area around it. Three different types of waterways are shown in Seminole. One is a bay. Seminole lies on Boca Ciega (**boe**-kah see-**ay**-gah) Bay.

Seminole also has several bayous. A **bayou** (**bie**-oo) is a stream of slow-moving water. A bayou flows into or out of another body of water such as a river or bay. In Seminole, the bayous are part of Boca Ciega Bay.

A third type of waterway in Seminole is a lake. A **lake** is a body of water surrounded by land. Find Lake Seminole on the map.

Section Review

Write your answers on a sheet of paper.
1. What are the three different types of waterways in Seminole?
2. What is a bayou?
3. What gulf, bay, bayou, or lake is near your home?

180

2 The People of Seminole

People have lived in the Seminole area for thousands of years. The warm weather, good soil, and food from the nearby ocean brought American Indians there long ago.

In the 1800's, other settlers began moving into the area. Like the American Indians, these settlers fished in the gulf waters. They hunted for food in nearby woods. They also began to farm.

In 1823, one of the first **citrus** farms in the area was started. Citrus trees are trees that bear certain kinds of fruit. Some citrus fruits are lemons, limes, oranges, and grapefruit. The warm, sunny weather of Seminole is perfect for growing citrus fruits.

Over the years, more farmers and their families moved into the area. The small town began to grow.

citrus

trees that bear certain kinds of fruit, such as lemons, limes, oranges, and grapefruit

In the late 1800's, another town was growing even faster. This town was called St. Petersburg. Tourists began to visit St. Petersburg to enjoy the warm weather. Hotels and restaurants were built to serve the tourists.

Then many people began to buy land in St. Petersburg so they could live there all the time. More businesses were started, and new stores were built. The town grew quickly. In 1892, St. Petersburg became a city.

Seminole and St. Petersburg are close to each other. But a bayou lies between them. It was difficult for the people from Seminole to visit the nearby city. A horse and wagon could cross the bayou, but only when the water was low. People could also travel by boat across the bayou. The other route between the two communities was all the way around the bayou. This was a long trip.

Traveling by boat in a bayou

Homes along the water, Seminole, Florida

In 1915, a bridge was built across the bayou. It connected St. Petersburg and Seminole. Travel between the two communities became easier. Many people from Seminole began visiting the city. They went there because St. Petersburg had many more stores and businesses than Seminole. People could find goods and services in the city that the small town of Seminole did not have.

In the 1950's, many people who had retired, or stopped working at jobs, began moving to St. Petersburg. They wanted to live in the warm climate. The city became more crowded. Apartments and houses became harder to find.

Soon many retired people began looking for homes in nearby Seminole. In Seminole, senior citizens could find apartments or houses to live in. Other people moved from St. Petersburg to Seminole too. Before long, houses and streets covered the farmland of Seminole.

A view of St. Petersburg, Florida

Slowly Seminole changed. It grew from a farming community to the suburban area it is today. People in Seminole use St. Petersburg in many ways. Many people have jobs in the city. People use city services, such as large hospitals and schools. They visit city museums, restaurants, and stores. Then they drive back across the bridge to their homes in Seminole.

Section Review

Write your answers on a sheet of paper.
1. How did a bridge help Seminole change and grow?
2. Give two reasons why the people of Seminole often travel to St. Petersburg.
3. List two reasons why you would live in a city. List two reasons why you would live in a suburb.

3 A Community Changes

Today many people who live in Seminole are retired senior citizens. Most of these people have moved to Seminole from the northern part of the United States. They live in apartments, houses, or mobile homes in and around Seminole.

Senior citizens in Seminole have set up many groups. These groups offer activities for their members. These activities include picnics, dances, art classes, and plays. There are also special clubs for people who used to live in the same state before they moved to Florida. These clubs have such names as Michigan Club or Ohio Club.

Some special services are provided for retired people. For example, bus routes are planned so that senior citizens can travel to nearby shopping malls. Restaurants and theaters in the area often charge less for senior citizens than for younger people.

Senior citizens looking at the records for a fund-raising activity

The senior citizens living in Seminole have helped to change their community. Groups of retired people have worked to improve Seminole by raising money to build a bigger library. Other groups have helped make the city more beautiful.

One group of senior citizens worked together to improve a main street, Seminole Boulevard. A **boulevard** is a wide street that is often lined with trees. Seminole Boulevard was once completely paved. The senior citizen group planted trees and grass down the middle of the boulevard.

The retired people of Seminole do not have to travel into St. Petersburg every day to go to work. They spend much of their time in their community. Many new businesses, such as clothing shops, restaurants, and golf courses, have opened in Seminole to serve retired people.

boulevard

a wide street often lined with trees

All of these new businesses need workers. Some of the people who have moved to Seminole are not retired. People come to Seminole to work in the new businesses. Younger families with children are making Seminole their home. With so many people of all ages moving into the area, Seminole keeps growing.

Section Review

Write your answers on a sheet of paper.
1. How have senior citizens in Seminole helped their community?
2. How have senior citizens helped bring younger families into Seminole?
3. Name two ways that a senior citizens' group can help its community.

Pittsburgh— A City of Industry

The city of Pittsburgh is in southwestern Pennsylvania. Pittsburgh's location has helped make it an industrial city. In this chapter, you will learn about products made in Pittsburgh.

At the end of this chapter, you should be able to:
- ○ Explain how Pittsburgh's location helped it grow.
- ○ Name the natural resources that are important to Pittsburgh.
- ● Read a road map.
- ○ Explain how Pittsburgh solved some of its problems.

1 Three-River City

Pittsburgh is not on an ocean or a bay, but it is still a harbor city. It is an inland harbor. It is located where the Allegheny (al-uh-**gay**-nee) River and the Monongahela (muh-nong-guh-**hee**-luh) River meet. These rivers join at Pittsburgh to form the Ohio River.

Look at the map. Find the place where the two rivers meet to form the third. This place is called a **fork.** Three Rivers Stadium is located at this fork. It is the home of Pittsburgh's baseball and football teams.

Besides waterways, other transportation routes meet in Pittsburgh. Airplanes fly in and out of Pittsburgh's airport. The map shows that Pittsburgh is near **interstate highways.** They connect communities in neighboring states. Railroads lead to and from Pittsburgh. How many railroad routes into Pittsburgh can you find on the map?

fork
a place where rivers meet

interstate highway
a main road that connects communities in neighboring states

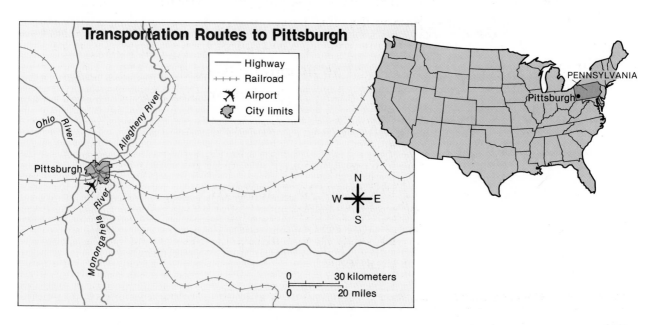

An important natural resource is found near Pittsburgh. This resource is coal. The coal mined near Pittsburgh is bituminous, or soft, coal.

As you have read, coal is a very useful mineral. It is burned to provide heat for homes. It is also used to provide power for industry. Many useful products, such as fuel, plastics, and nylon, are made from coal. Pittsburgh uses coal in one of its biggest industries, steel production.

Good transportation and nearby natural resources are very important to Pittsburgh. They have helped this community grow.

A worker in a steel plant

Section Review

Write your answers on a sheet of paper.
1. Name four kinds of transportation in Pittsburgh.
2. Why is coal important to Pittsburgh?
3. What natural resources are important to your community? Tell why they are important.

2 Gateway City

In 1758, the British captured a French fort at the fork of the Allegheny and Monongahela rivers. They named it Fort Pitt, after a British leader named William Pitt.

A settlement began around Fort Pitt. This settlement, named Pittsburgh, became a center for boat building. In Pittsburgh, people from the east could get boats and begin their journey west. They were traveling westward to explore new areas of the country. Travelers began their journey in Pittsburgh because of its location on three rivers. The area became known as the Gateway to the West.

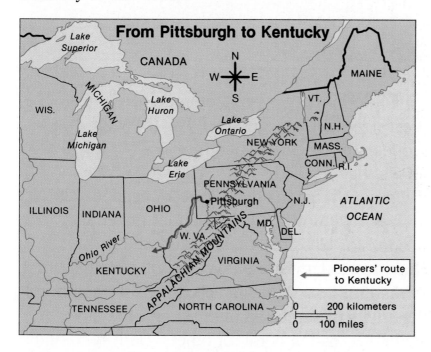

These travelers were **pioneers,** or people who are the first to settle in a place. They traveled by boat down the Ohio River into Kentucky. Some pioneers stayed in Kentucky. Others continued their journey west.

pioneer
a person who is the first to settle in a place

Riverboat travel in the early 1800's

People in the growing communities in the West needed many goods. It was easy for pioneers to reach Pittsburgh by boat to buy the goods they needed.

One of the goods that pioneers needed was glass for windows. Two important materials needed for glassmaking are sand and **limestone.** Limestone is a kind of rock that was formed millions of years ago. It was formed from the shells of some sea animals and the tiny skeletons, called coral, of others. Both sand and limestone can be found near Pittsburgh. By 1797, people in Pittsburgh had started a glassmaking industry to serve the pioneers in the West. Today Pittsburgh is still a glassmaking center.

limestone
rock that was formed millions of years ago from the shells of some sea animals and the tiny skeletons, called coral, of others

The materials needed to make iron are iron ore, coal, and limestone. All three are found near Pittsburgh. Pittsburgh became known for making iron. People began calling Pittsburgh the Iron City.

Many goods that people needed, such as stoves, pots, and tools, were made from iron. But people in Pittsburgh wanted to make a new, stronger material to use for railroad tracks. The new, stronger material they made was called steel. Steel is made from the same materials as iron, but a different kind of furnace is used to make steel. All of the materials needed to make steel are available near Pittsburgh. Steelmaking became a very big and important industry in Pittsburgh.

Natural resources helped Pittsburgh's industries grow. So did new forms of transportation. Look at the **time line,** or graph that shows periods of time. It shows three ways to get from place to place. Why do you think good transportation helped Pittsburgh's industries grow?

time line
a graph that shows periods of time

New Forms of Transportation, 1807-1851

1807	1834	1851
Invention of the steamboat	Pennsylvania Canal links Pittsburgh with the East	Railroad reaches Pittsburgh

193

immigrant
a person who comes from another country to live in a new land

By 1900, Pittsburgh was an important industrial city. Many people from other countries came to Pittsburgh to look for jobs in the new iron and steel factories. These people were called **immigrants.**

Andrew Carnegie (**car**-nuh-gee) was an immigrant from Scotland. He settled in Pittsburgh. Carnegie started a small company that made railroad cars. As a businessman, he knew how important the iron and steel industries were. At first, he started some small steel mills. He used his mills to supply steel to build bridges, factories, and railroads. Later he bought other steel mills as well as iron-ore and coal fields. Then his mills had everything they needed to make steel. His small mills grew into large factories. Soon Carnegie's factories produced most of the steel used in the United States.

Andrew Carnegie became very rich. But he wanted to share his money. So he decided to give a lot of his money away. Carnegie used his money to build schools, hospitals, parks, churches, museums, and concert halls. He also paid for more than 3,000 public libraries.

Andrew Carnegie gave some of his money to museums, like the Metropolitan Museum in New York City.

Industrial cities such as Pittsburgh helped the United States become an industrial nation. Steel from Pittsburgh's many factories supplies many other industries all over the United States. These industries use steel for factory equipment and for parts to make many other products. Jet airliners, railroad cars and tracks, and many other things are made from steel. The pictures on this page show some of the other products that are made from steel.

Section Review

Reading a Road Map

road map
a guide to roads and highways, showing the ways to go from one place to another

boundary
the edge of a particular place, such as a town, city, or playground

Road maps are special maps that show roads and highways. People driving cars, trucks, buses, and even riding bicycles may use road maps to find the best way to go from one place to another.

Towns and cities are shown on road maps. A dot or circle may be used to show a town or city. The size of the dot or circle tells you whether the town or city is large or small. The names of big towns are often shown in large dark letters. If a city is very large, its **boundaries,** or edges, may be shown. The color green shows the city limits of Pittsburgh on the map on the next page.

Road maps also show rivers and lakes. Airports and railroads may be shown as well. Find this airport symbol on the map: ✈

Road maps use lines of different colors and thicknesses to show roads and highways. Thin black lines usually show the small roads used for travel between local communities. Thick black lines often show the larger highways. These roads connect towns and cities within each state. Thick red lines are often used to show large interstate highways. Interstate highways are built by the national government for travel through different states.

Highways are numbered to help guide people. Interstate highways running east and west have even numbers. Interstate highways running north and south have odd numbers.

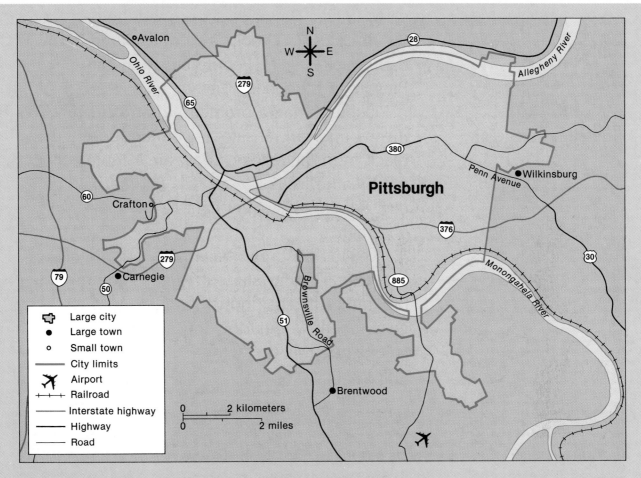

Practice Your Skills

1. Which place is larger, Carnegie or Crafton?
2. What kind of road passes through Avalon? What is its number?
3. If you wanted to go from Carnegie to Wilkinsburg, what interstate highways could you use for most of the trip? In which direction would you be traveling?
4. Near what town do highways 376 and 30 meet?

3 Pittsburgh's New Look

Pittsburgh's industries grew quickly in the early 1900's. Factories soon lined the banks of the three rivers. Smoke and dirt poured from their smokestacks. People began to call Pittsburgh the Smoky City.

Pittsburgh had a problem, **air pollution.** This means unclean, unsafe air. Buildings turned black from the smoky, sooty air. People could not breathe well. The air was dark during the day. Pittsburgh's street lights were kept on day and night.

In 1946, Pittsburgh began to work on this problem. The city started a smoke-control program. Citizens, industries, and the city government worked together. Many factories put smoke controls on factory equipment to stop the pollution.

air pollution
unclean, unsafe air

Noon in Pittsburgh, January, 1944

By the 1950's, Pittsburgh's air was cleaner. People started programs to clean Pittsburgh's buildings. New highways and bridges were built. Streets were widened. Pittsburgh had a new look.

Pittsburgh is a city that has continued to grow and change. Many industries have made Pittsburgh their headquarters. One of their reasons for doing so is Pittsburgh's location on three rivers.

New apartment buildings have been built. Old buildings have been restored. New schools and community programs have been started. Pittsburgh is still an important industrial community in the United States.

(above) Restoring a house in Pittsburgh

(left) A summer concert near the Allegheny River

Section Review

Write your answers on a sheet of paper.
1. Why was Pittsburgh called the Smoky City?
2. What did the people of Pittsburgh do to help solve the pollution problem?
3. What are some ways a community can prevent pollution?

A City Festival The long, cold winter is over. Buds sprout on bushes and trees. Spring is here! People all over the world hold festivals to celebrate the coming of spring.

Cambridge, Massachusetts, is a city located next to Boston. The people of Cambridge celebrate the coming of spring with a large festival. It is called the Cambridge River Festival. It begins on a Sunday and lasts for one week. The festival starts on the common, or town square.

Dancers, musicians, and actors perform for the gathering crowds.

The festival moves to a different neighborhood each day during the festival week. Special events are planned for each neighborhood. Many Portuguese Americans live in East Cambridge. On the day the festival moves to East Cambridge, people listen to a lively band that plays Portuguese music.

There is something for everyone at the Cambridge River Festival.

People walk from one event to the next. They may watch a dance performance. Or they may watch a parade. Many people come in costume. Children can see plays put on just for them or have their faces painted in bright colors.

On Saturday, the last day of the festival, the people of Cambridge wake up to a wonderful sight. In the middle of the night, thousands of balloons have been tied to door-knobs, lamp posts, and hydrants. Cambridge is filled with color. At noon, two parades march to the banks of the Charles River. Stages are set up, and actors and musicians perform as people walk by. A band plays on a barge floating down the river.

The festival continues into the night. Finally, a musical group plays one last song, and the festival is over. But spring has been celebrated in a grand way by the people of Cambridge.

Word Work

Write the sentences below on a sheet of paper. Fill in the blanks with the correct words from the list.

bayou   fork   immigrant   metropolitan

1. An _____ is a person who comes from another country to live in a new land.
2. A _____ is a stream of slow-moving water that flows into or out of another body of water.
3. A _____ area is a city and the communities around it.
4. A _____ is a place where rivers meet.

Knowing the Facts

Write your answers on a sheet of paper.
1. How did San Francisco solve its transportation problems?
2. What improvements can senior citizens' groups make in a community?
3. What resources helped Pittsburgh grow?
4. What problem did industry cause in Pittsburgh?

Using What You Know

Choose one of the following activities to do. Follow the instructions given here.
1. Write a flow chart that shows how your class spends a school day.
2. Make a list of five ways your school can help prevent or clean up pollution.

Skills Practice

Use the following map and map key to answer the questions below. Write your answers on a sheet of paper.

1. Which community is larger, Catlettsburg or Huntington?
2. What interstate highway would you take to get from Huntington to the closest airport? In what direction would you be traveling?
3. What road would take you from Bradrick to Chesapeake?

Your Community

Most communities have changed since they were first settled. Some changes have made things better. Some have caused problems.

What are some of the changes you have noticed in your community? How have these changes helped you and your community?

UNIT
5

Communities in Other Lands

The pictures on these pages show communities in other lands. The pictures show some things that all communities need. They also show some things you may not have seen before.

In this unit, you will learn about four communities in other countries. You will see some of the ways communities all over the world are the same. You will also learn how they are different.

CHAPTER 15

London— A City of History

More than 7 million people live in London, England. This large city is nearly 2,000 years old. Many important events have taken place in London. London is also a center of industry.

Look at the picture on this page. These soldiers are guards at Buckingham Palace. This beautiful palace is one of the homes of England's queens and kings.

At the end of this chapter, you should be able to:

○ Tell why the Thames River is important to London.

○ Compare the governments of Great Britain and the United States.

● Use a globe to study hemispheres, continents, and the earth's axis.

1 A Look at London

England is on one of the islands that make up Great Britain. Look at the map. What other countries are on the same island? What bodies of water surround England?

Now find London on the map. This city is on the Thames (**temz**) River. Ships sail up the Thames to a harbor in London.

London's harbor is one of the busiest in the world. Ships come and go every day loaded with goods.

Warm winds from the Atlantic Ocean usually keep Great Britain's temperatures mild in winter and not very hot in summer. These winds also bring a lot of rain and fog. In fact, London is known for its fog.

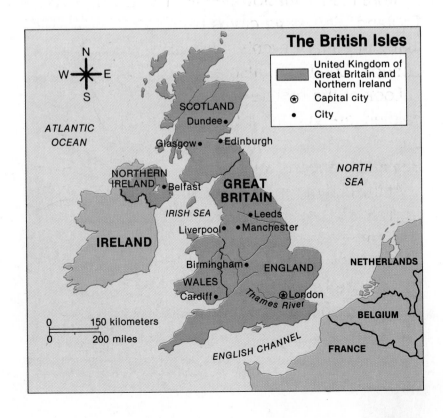

London is a city of many different sections. Some sections are centers for certain kinds of work. Other sections of the city are where people live.

Look at the map key. Then find the section where detectives work. Where would you go to see a play? Where could you visit a newspaper office?

The center of London is an area with shops, businesses, theaters, museums, and government buildings. Bond Street is a famous shopping area in the center of London. Find Bond Street on the map. Name three parks near this shopping area.

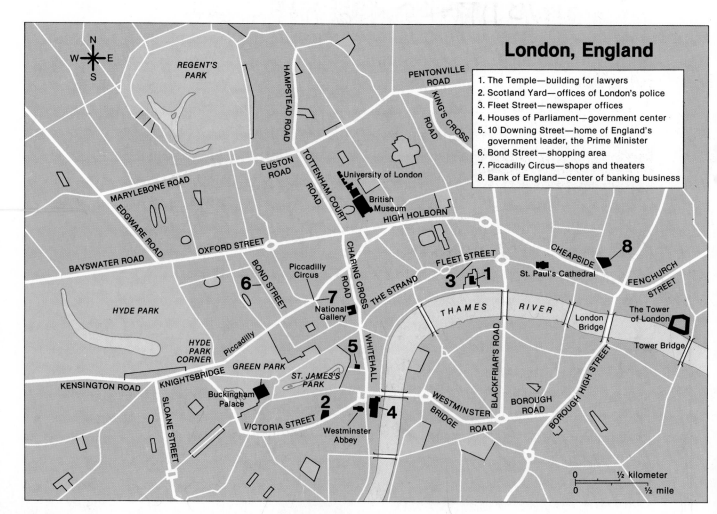

London, England

1. The Temple—building for lawyers
2. Scotland Yard—offices of London's police
3. Fleet Street—newspaper offices
4. Houses of Parliament—government center
5. 10 Downing Street—home of England's government leader, the Prime Minister
6. Bond Street—shopping area
7. Piccadilly Circus—shops and theaters
8. Bank of England—center of banking business

The picture on this page shows a part of London where people live. Many of the houses are for two families. Almost every house has a garden.

People who live outside the city's center need good transportation to get to work. Some people use the Underground, London's subway system. Some ride double-decker buses to work. Others use cars. Some people even ride bikes!

London is the center of England's railway system. There are eight railroad stations in the city. London's postal system also has a railroad system. This railroad carries mail around the city—underground!

Section Review

Write your answers on a sheet of paper.
1. What river runs through London?
2. Name three ways people get around London.
3. Name two sections in London a tourist might want to visit.

2 Life in London

monarchy

a government headed by a king or queen

Parliament

a group of people who make the laws of Great Britain

London is a city that has a long and famous history. You can see reminders of the past all over the city. The symbol of a crown appears on many things. The crown stands for the British **monarchy** (**mahn**-ahr-kee). A monarchy is a government headed by a king or queen. The British people have had a king or queen for more than 1,000 years. Today the head of Great Britain is a queen. She is important to the people as a symbol of the nation. Her name is Queen Elizabeth.

The laws of Great Britain are made by **Parliament** (**pahr**-luh-munt). Parliament has two parts, the House of Commons and the

(left) Big Ben and the Houses of Parliament   (below) The royal family at the wedding of Prince Charles and Lady Diana, July 1981; the Queen is in the second row, fourth from the left

House of Lords. Members of the House of Commons are elected. Members of the House of Lords are members for life. Membership in the House of Lords is passed down from parents to children.

Parliament is headed by a **prime minister.** The prime minister leads the government.

The lawmakers of Great Britain meet in buildings called the Houses of Parliament. A famous clock called Big Ben booms the time from a tower on top of these buildings.

Nearby is Westminster Abbey. This church is where the kings and queens of England are crowned. Many kings and queens are married there. And often they—and other famous people—are buried there.

Tourists like to visit the Tower of London. Part of it was built over 900 years ago. Through the ages the tower has been used as a fort, a palace, and a prison. Today the tower is a museum. The beautiful crown jewels are on display there. These jewels are sometimes worn by kings and queens of England.

prime minister
the leader of Parliament and head of the British government

(above) A knight on horseback, part of the armor collection in the Tower of London
(below) Westminster Abbey with Big Ben at the left

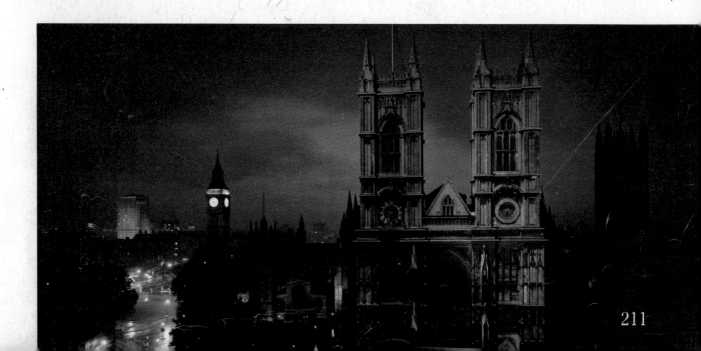

Two Kinds of English

American		British
Truck		Lorry
Police Officer		Bobby
Gas		Petrol
Baby Carriage		Pram
Cookie		Biscuit

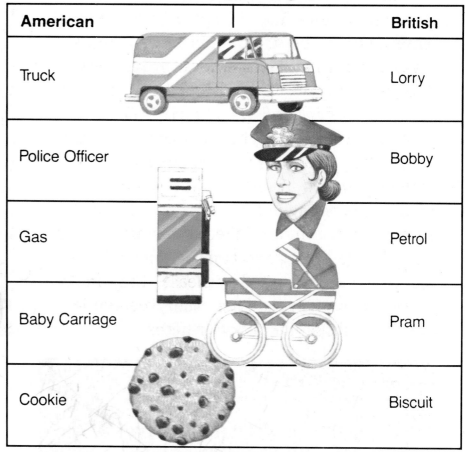

In some ways, life in London is like life in many cities in the United States. In other ways, it is different.

People in England and the United States speak the same language—English. But some words are used differently. Here is an example: "Let's have fish and chips." Do you know what that sentence means? Fish and chips is a favorite dish in England. It is what Americans call fried fish and French-fried potatoes.

In England, "queuing up" means "lining up." In London, people buy fruit at the "greengrocer," or ice cream at the "sweet shop." The chart on this page tells you some other English words that American people and British people use differently.

People in both the United States and England drink tea. But teatime is a special custom for the British. Every afternoon at four o'clock, many people stop what they are doing to have tea. This custom goes back to the 1600's, when tea was first brought to England from Asia.

A woman in one of the pictures on this page is following a famous London custom. She is making a speech at Hyde Park. The freedom to make speeches in public is important to the British. People in the United States feel the same way. People in England and the United States are free to worship as they please. They are free to live and work where they like. Freedom is part of everyday life in both nations.

(above) Speaker's Corner, Hyde Park, London   (left) Teatime in England

Section Review

Write your answers on a sheet of paper.
1. What language is spoken in England?
2. Write a sentence using a British English word.
3. Name one difference between the government of the United States and the government of Great Britain.

Using a Globe

ocean
a large body of salt water that covers much of the earth's surface

continent
one of the seven large bodies of land on the earth's surface

Suppose you went into space and looked back at the earth. It would look round—nearly as round as a ball.

The round shape of the earth can be shown by a model, called a globe. A globe also shows the shape of the earth's water and land areas.

On a globe, you can clearly see the shapes of the earth's large bodies of water, called **oceans.** There are four oceans on the earth's surface— the Atlantic, Pacific, Arctic, and Indian oceans. On a globe, they are colored blue. You can also see the shapes of the earth's large areas of land, called **continents.**

There are seven continents on the earth. You can see parts of two of them in the pictures on this page—North America and South America. The other continents are Europe, Asia, Africa, Australia, and Antarctica. You cannot see these continents on this page. Because a globe is round like the earth, you can only see one half of it at a time. The other continents are on the half of the globe that you cannot see.

(above) The earth as seen from space   (right) Looking at a globe

Another way of saying "half of the earth" is to use the word **hemisphere.** "Hemi" means half. "Sphere" means ball or globe.

Suppose you could slice through the earth from the North Pole to the South Pole. You would get two hemispheres. You cannot cut the earth into two halves, of course. But you can talk about the earth's two halves. One half is called the Western Hemisphere. The other is called the Eastern Hemisphere.

Look at the drawings on this page. You can see that the continents of North America and South America are in the Western Hemisphere. Europe, Asia, Africa, and Australia are in the Eastern Hemisphere. Antarctica is in both the Eastern and the Western hemispheres.

hemisphere
half of the earth

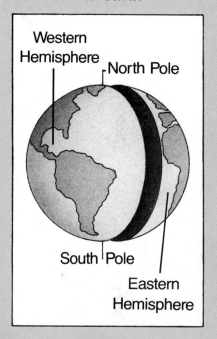

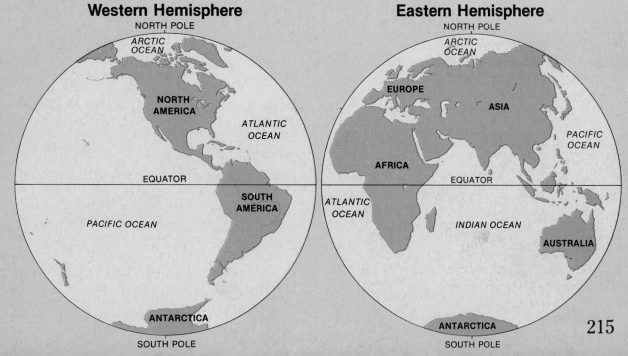

Western Hemisphere

NORTH POLE
ARCTIC OCEAN
NORTH AMERICA
ATLANTIC OCEAN
EQUATOR
SOUTH AMERICA
PACIFIC OCEAN
ANTARCTICA
SOUTH POLE

Eastern Hemisphere

NORTH POLE
ARCTIC OCEAN
EUROPE
ASIA
PACIFIC OCEAN
AFRICA
EQUATOR
ATLANTIC OCEAN
INDIAN OCEAN
AUSTRALIA
ANTARCTICA
SOUTH POLE

215

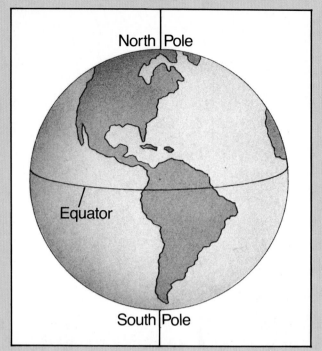

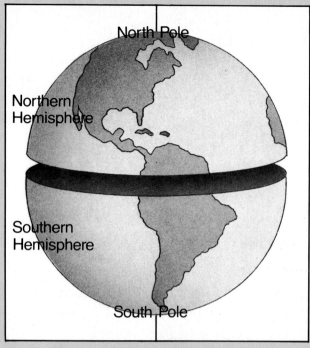

equator

an imaginary line that runs east and west around the middle of the earth

Another way to divide the earth is along the **equator.** The equator is an imaginary line that runs east and west around the middle of the earth. It is halfway between the North and South poles.

If you could slice through the earth at the equator, everything to the north would be in the Northern Hemisphere. Everything to the south would be in the Southern Hemisphere. Some continents, like South America, would be sliced apart.

You can see that North America is north of the equator. It lies in the Northern Hemisphere. Look at the drawings on page 215. Where is Europe? It, too, is in the Northern Hemisphere.

When you divide the earth at the equator, the continents of Europe and North America are on the same side of the earth. When you divide the earth from pole to pole, these two continents are on opposite sides. Every spot on the earth can be said to be in two hemispheres.

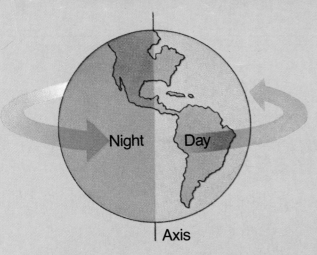

Night Day

Axis

Sun

A globe shows the round shape of the earth. A globe can also show the way the earth turns on its **axis.** An axis is an imaginary line that cuts through the center of the earth. It goes from the North Pole to the South Pole. The earth turns, or **rotates,** around this axis every 24 hours. The globe on page 214 has an axis. So does the diagram of the earth on this page.

If the earth did not turn, one hemisphere would always face the sun. It would always be daytime in that hemisphere. It would always be night in the other hemisphere. Because the earth rotates, the dark side moves into the sun's light, and, somewhere in the world, a new day begins.

axis
an imaginary straight line going through the earth from the North Pole to the South Pole
rotate
to turn or spin

___ Practice Your Skills ___

1. Name the continents in the Eastern Hemisphere.
2. What continents lie in both the Northern Hemisphere and the Southern Hemisphere?
3. In which two hemispheres is the United States?
4. When it is daytime across the Western Hemisphere, where is it night?

16 Seto— A Village in Japan

On the Inland Sea, Seto, Japan

A timeless concert
On the dawn-lit ocean as
The wind plays its drums.

The poem you have just read is called haiku (hie-**koo**). Haiku is a form of Japanese poetry. Haiku poems are word pictures about nature.

In this chapter, you will read about the people of Japan. You will read about a small Japanese fishing village called Seto (**set**-toe).

At the end of this chapter, you should be able to:
○ Tell how sea currents affect climate in Seto.
○ Explain why the sea is important to the people of Seto.
○ Name some customs of the people of Seto.

1 Island Nation

Japan is made up of four big islands and about 3,000 smaller ones. The village of Seto is on a big island called Shikoku (**shee**-koe-koo). Find Shikoku on the map.

Seto is located on the Inland Sea. A warm ocean **current** flows along Shikoku's coasts. A current is the steady flow of water in one direction. If the water in a current is warm, the air over the water is warmed too. Seto's climate is warm because of warm sea currents.

Seto's summers are long and hot. Winters are mild like winters in parts of North Carolina.

current
the steady flow of water in one direction

SOVIET UNION

CHINA

HOKKAIDO

Sapporo

NORTH KOREA

SEA OF JAPAN

SOUTH KOREA

HONSHU

Nagoya

JAPAN

Tokyo

Kyoto

INLAND SEA · Osaka

Seto · Matsuyama

SHIKOKU

KYUSHU

PACIFIC OCEAN

RYUKYU ISLANDS

0   200 kilometers
0   150 miles

⊛   Capital city
•   City
○   Small town

tradition
a custom followed over a long period of time

More than 113 million people live in Japan. Most people live in communities along the coasts of Japan's islands. Some cities, such as the capital city of Tokyo, are big and very crowded. Other communities, such as Seto, are small and quiet. Look at the pictures. Which one shows people following **traditions?** Traditions are customs followed over a long period of time.

The photographs show that Japan is both a modern nation and a traditional nation. Japan is modern because it has more industry than most other nations in the world. But Japan is also a nation that follows old customs. One custom is called the tea ceremony. In this ceremony, tea is prepared and served following special rules.

(above) Japanese tea ceremony   (right) Downtown Tokyo, Japan

Section Review

Write your answers on a sheet of paper.
1. How do sea currents affect Seto's climate?
2. Name one way Tokyo and Seto are alike. Name one way these communities are different.
3. What custom do people in Seto and London share?

2 A Fishing Village

About 5,000 people live in the village of Seto. Most families earn a living from the sea. The fishing people of Seto use large nets or fishing poles to fish in the nearby waters. They fish from small ships called trawlers. The trawlers are owned by fishing companies.

People in Japan make fishing poles from the stalks of the bamboo plant. This plant has a strong, hollow stem. It is used by Japanese people for many things, including furniture and tools. Bamboo strips are also woven together to make fishing baskets. The baskets are used to carry the day's catch from the trawlers.

The fishing people of Seto go to sea in all kinds of weather. Abalone (ab-uh-**loe**-nee), shrimp, squid, and tuna are caught in the Inland Sea. These kinds of seafood are all good to eat.

Fixing a fishing net

(left) The boats of fishing
people on the Inland Sea,
Japan   (right) Octopus in the
fish market, Tokyo, Japan

Each family that fishes has its own small boat.
This boat is used to travel back and forth
between the shore and the trawler. At the end of
the day, fishing people bring their catch to
shore. Some of the fish is sold in the village.

Most of the catch goes to fish markets in big
cities. Fresh fish from a small village like Seto
can be in a city market by early morning each
day. This is possible because the communities
in Japan are connected to each other by a good
railroad system. The transportation system helps
people to sell their catch from the sea. The
transportation system also helps people to get
goods from other parts of Japan.

Fishing is an important industry in Japan.
Japanese people eat a lot of fish. Japan also
sells canned and frozen fish to other countries.
Do you like tuna fish? The tuna fish you eat
probably comes from Japan. Each year Japan
sells thousands of kilograms (pounds) of fish
the United States.

Seto is near the city of Matsuyama (maht-soo-**yah**-muh). In Matsuyama, people live in apartment buildings. They work in banks, factories, and other businesses. For fun, they go to movies, sports events, or restaurants. Some children wear the traditional clothing of Japan, but many wear clothes that look like yours.

In Seto, life is more traditional than life in the city. Villagers there live in small houses. Sliding paper doors separate the rooms inside.

People all over Japan follow many of the same customs. Straw mats called tatami (tah-**tah**-mee) cover the floors. Before entering a house, people take off their shoes. They sit on cushions on the floor. At night, quilts are unfolded on the floor for sleeping.

At home, many Japanese people wear long robes of cotton or silk called kimonos (kih-**moe**-noze). A kimono is tied at the waist with a sash called an obi (**oe**-bee). In Seto, some people wear kimonos at home and at work. In large cities, most people wear kimonos only at home. They wear clothes like people in the United States outside the home.

(left) Taking a nap on a tatami   (right) A sliding panel made of wood and paper is used as a door in a traditional Japanese house.

223

In a village, there are not as many places to go as in a city. For example, Seto has no large department stores or restaurants. Instead, most people have meals at home. But whether they live in villages or cities, Japanese people like to eat some of the same dishes. Rice, raw fish, and seaweed are favorite foods throughout Japan. Tea is the favorite drink.

One festival that Japanese children enjoy is called *Tanabata* (tah-nah-**bah**-tah). During this festival, boys and girls make a tree out of bamboo. Then they write haiku and other poems. The children hang their poems on the tree for everyone to read. It is a special way to share their thoughts.

A child writing in Japanese, using a brush and ink

Section Review

Write your answers on a sheet of paper.
1. Name two reasons why fish are important in Seto.
2. Name two traditions that people in Seto follow.
3. How is your home different from a house in Seto? How is it the same?

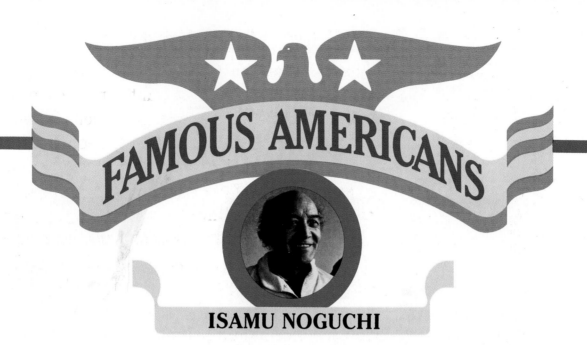

FAMOUS AMERICANS

ISAMU NOGUCHI

Stone, metal, and wood are some materials Isamu Noguchi (**ih**-sah-moo noe-**goo**-chee) uses in his work. He is a sculptor. He uses these materials to show us the shapes of things.

Noguchi was born in California. His mother was American and his father Japanese. When he was two years old, he moved with his parents to Japan. Even when he was very young, he noticed the shapes of the things he saw. Noguchi wanted to make sculptures as beautiful as the real things he saw around him.

Noguchi returned to the United States when he was 17. He decided to go to art school. There he could learn how to make sculptures. In 1927, he went to Paris to study with Constantin Brancusi (kon-stun-**teen** bran-**koo**-zee), a famous artist. When he went back to the United States, Noguchi's sculptures made him famous.

Noguchi designs playgrounds, gardens, and bridges, as well as wonderful sculptures. His sculptures can be seen in the United States and in countries throughout the world. Their shapes might surprise you. One sculpture, called "Vertical Man," is a huge block of stone balanced on a piece of wood. It might remind you of a person. It might remind you of something else. But if it makes you think, feel, or wonder, then Isamu Noguchi would be proud.

CHAPTER 17

Hanita— A Kibbutz in Israel

Worker cutting back a banana plant, Hanita, Israel

A kibbutz (kih-**boohts**) is a special kind of community in the country of Israel. Living on a kibbutz means sharing many things with the other people who live there.

In this chapter you will read about Hanita (hah-**nee**-tah), a kibbutz in northern Israel. You will learn how everyone helps with the work of the kibbutz, and how the kibbutz serves the needs of everyone in it.

At the end of this chapter, you should be able to:

○ Describe how work on a kibbutz is shared.
○ Describe the land and climate around Hanita.
○ List the kinds of work done at Hanita.
○ Describe how a kibbutz is governed.

1 The Kibbutz Community

A **kibbutz** is a community in Israel where all the people live and work as a group. The word kibbutz means "group" in Hebrew. Hebrew is the official language of Israel. There are more than 250 kibbutzim (kih-boohts-**eem**) in Israel today. There are kibbutzim in all parts of the country.

People work and play together on a kibbutz. Each person helps the group by doing some kind of work on the kibbutz. The group, in turn, takes care of the needs of each person.

This system of group living works best for small groups. Thirty people may live on a new farm kibbutz. The largest kibbutzim have about 2,000 people. On the average kibbutz, there are 400 to 500 people.

kibbutz
a community in Israel where all the people live and work as a group

Map showing Israel and surrounding region including Lebanon, Syria, Jordan, Saudi Arabia, and Egypt. Cities and places labeled: Hanita, Haifa, Deganya, Lake Kinneret (Sea of Galilee), Tel Aviv, Jerusalem, Dead Sea. Bodies of water: Mediterranean Sea, Jordan R. Scale: 0–60 kilometers, 0–50 miles. Legend: Capital city, City or town, Occupied land.

Hanita is a kibbutz of 450 people. It is located high in the hills of northern Israel, near the border with Lebanon. Of the 450 people who live in the settlement, 300 are kibbutz members. The rest are children of members, or retired parents who stay with a member, or visiting students and workers.

The community must take care of almost all its own needs. It is not closely tied to other communities. Hanita is on a small road. Only three buses come up the road each day. The nearest large town is Haifa (**hie**-fuh). Haifa is more than 50 kilometers (31 miles) from Hanita.

Hanita can take care of most of its own needs because it is in a good location. It sits in a beautiful valley, with mountains all around. Water from springs and deep wells keeps orchards and fields green during the summer.

The weather at Hanita is mild compared to most climates of the world. There is some rain in winter, but rarely snow. The summers are warm, but it is rarely hotter than 35°C (95°F). The high hills keep Hanita cooler than the dry, southern part of Israel.

A local bus stops at Hanita.

Workers on their way to the orchards

Hanita's climate is good for growing crops. The mild winters mean tropical fruits can be grown. Large groves of citrus trees produce hundreds of tons of oranges, lemons, and grapefruit every year. Avocados and bananas are also important crops on the kibbutz. Many of these fruits are sold in Europe and in the United States. Turkeys are also raised on the kibbutz. Cotton grown on the kibbutz is sent to mills in other parts of the country. These mills make the cotton into cloth.

Smaller crops of flowers and wheat are also grown at Hanita. All of the money from the sale of the crops is used by the kibbutz to care for its people.

The kibbutz must have a way to bring in money during poor farm years. Sometimes frost damages the fruit, or prices are low when the crops are ready to be sold. The kibbutz must earn money from some industry other than farming.

Worker in the tool factory at Hanita

To solve this problem, the kibbutz has a factory as well as farms. The factory produces fine tools for drilling and cutting metal. There is a great demand for these well-made tools. Factories all over the world want to use them because they last longer than other tools.

In some years, the sale of tools brings in more money than the sale of Hanita's farm crops. But this does not make the tool makers more important than the farm workers on the kibbutz. Each person is equally important.

The fields and factory at Hanita do not belong to any one person. Every part of the kibbutz belongs to every member. And the kibbutz is "home" to all who live there.

Section Review

Write your answers on a sheet of paper.
1. What is the official language of Israel?
2. How is summer weather in Hanita different from that of most of Israel?
3. Name four fruits grown in Hanita's orchards.
4. Who owns the factory and the farmland at Hanita?

2 Life on the Kibbutz

The first kibbutz was started on a farm at Deganya (deh-**gahn**-yah), just south of Lake Kinneret (kih-**neh**-ret). This lake was known as the Sea of Galilee (**gal**-ih-lee) in ancient times. A group of Jewish settlers took over responsibility for the farm. They wanted to create a new kind of community that would be almost like a large family. This was in 1909, when Deganya was a part of the Arab country of Palestine. The state of Israel was established almost 40 years later.

From the beginning, the people of Deganya shared all work on the farm equally. They also shared all the money they earned. No one person owned more or less. They used no money among themselves. They all worked to build up the kibbutz. They had to work very hard to make the farm produce crops. The soil was poor, and earlier farmers had let much of it wash away. But the new kibbutz farmers worked together so well that their farm began to improve.

Near Lake Kinneret

An early kibbutz

Other Jews came to Palestine from other parts of the world. They started several new kibbutzim. Many of them had to struggle for years to establish vegetable, fruit, dairy, and poultry farms. Sometimes there were failures. Some of the people left their farms and went to other countries. Sometimes there were fights with the Arabs who lived in the area around a kibbutz.

But the kibbutzniks (kih-**boohts**-niks), as the people of a kibbutz are called, did not give up. The men, women, and children all worked hard. The kibbutzim grew stronger. When Israel became an independent nation in 1948, the kibbutzim grew food for the new country. They also helped protect Israel's borders from hostile neighbor countries.

The kibbutzniks had worked hard to make the kibbutzim grow. They were also ready to work hard for the Jewish nation of Israel.

After 1948, the kibbutzim increased in number. The government gave money to help start new settlements. Soon there were so many farms that the country was running short of water and farmland. Israel also needed manufactured goods. Many of the kibbutzim began to produce goods such as furniture, electronic and electric equipment, and tools for farms and factories.

Hanita was a typical growing kibbutz. It began as a farm and border guardpost in 1939. A tool factory was started later.

People from many different lands settled at Hanita. The first settlers were from southern Israel, Romania, Austria, and Germany. Later, people came from France and northern Africa.

You might hear people at Hanita speaking French, German, or English today. But they have all learned to speak Hebrew.

Hanita in the early 1940's

A kibbutz meeting at Hanita

Once a week the members of the kibbutz go to a large meeting. There they discuss all important problems. They vote on ways to try to solve the problems. They hear the reports of committees, which take care of the day-to-day business of the kibbutz. Everyone has an equal voice in making decisions for the kibbutz.

The people of the kibbutz are together for much more than their weekly meetings. Many eat together in the shared dining hall. They all use the same laundry, the same medical office, the same supply store, and the same school.

Most babies and young children of the kibbutz live together in a special children's house. Several men and women also live in the house and take care of the children day and night. The children see their parents several times a day. But they often have as strong a feeling for the kibbutz group as they do for their family.

The children play, work, and study together. They learn to share all their toys. As adults, they will all do an equal share of work on the kibbutz. They may work in the garden, in the dining hall, on the farm, or in the factory. Sharing with their fellow kibbutzniks is their whole way of life—the group life of the kibbutz.

In the children's house at Hanita

Section Review

Write your answers on a sheet of paper.
1. Where was the first kibbutz started?
2. Who makes the decisions of the kibbutz?
3. How are young children cared for on a kibbutz?

CHAPTER 18 Nairobi— A City in Africa

The picture on this page shows the busy, modern city of Nairobi (nie-**roe**-bee). Nairobi is the capital of Kenya (**ken**-yuh), a nation in Africa.

Nairobi is the center of industry and trade for Kenya and the nations around it. Nairobi is also a city visited by tourists from around the world.

At the end of this chapter, you should be able to:

○ Describe the climate in Nairobi.
○ Describe an industry in Nairobi.
○ Tell why Nairobi is a leader for other communities in Kenya.

1 Mile-High City

Nairobi is in south-central Kenya. Kenya is in east-central Africa. You can find Kenya and Nairobi on the map on this page. What countries is Kenya near?

Nairobi is on very high land, where the air is dry and cool. Some people call Nairobi the mile-high city. In these highlands, there is plenty of sunshine. The climate is good for growing crops. The climate is also very pleasant. The pleasant climate is one reason why many people in Kenya live in Nairobi.

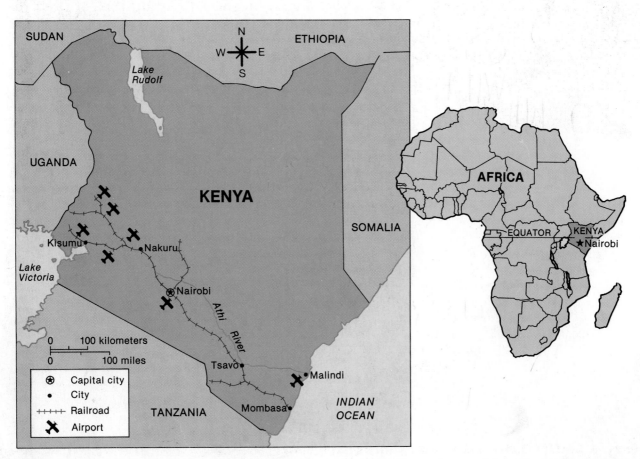

The highlands around Nairobi have rich soil. The area gets plenty of rain, and the growing season lasts all year. Many of Kenya's farms are in the highlands. Some of the main crops are coffee, tea, corn, wheat, and sugarcane.

Farmers bring their crops to Nairobi. The farmers sell their crops to companies that make food products. For example, wheat is used to make bread. Making crops into food products is called **food processing.** Food processing is one of Nairobi's biggest industries.

food processing
making crops into food products

Nairobi is also a center of transportation. Crops and goods are sent by rail from Nairobi to all parts of Kenya. Crops are shipped by boat to other nations too. Mombasa (mom-**bah**-suh) is Kenya's main port. What ocean is Mombasa on?

Harvesting tea in Kenya

Section Review

Write your answers on a sheet of paper.
1. What two resources help Kenya's farmers?
2. What crops are grown around Nairobi?
3. What happens to the crops that are brought to Nairobi?

2 A Fast-Growing City

In 1880, herders would gather at a waterhole so their animals could drink. These herders were members of a **tribe** called the Masai (muh-**sie**). A tribe is a group of people with the same relatives, language, and customs. The Masai had a special name for the waterhole. It was "Nairobi." In the Masai language, this means cool waters.

Then people came from Great Britain to settle in Kenya. They wanted to develop the land's resources. The British started a settlement at Nairobi. They built a railroad to link Nairobi to Mombasa. Many people from Great Britain came to live in Nairobi. People from other nations, such as India, came to settle in Nairobi too. The community grew quickly.

Today Nairobi is one of the biggest cities in east-central Africa. It is the capital of Kenya. People from Kenya's neighboring nations come to Nairobi to meet and trade. Many government office buildings are located in Nairobi.

tribe
a group of people with the same relatives, language, and customs

A Masai herder giving water to the cattle

Today people of many backgrounds live in Nairobi. People from 40 African tribes live there. People from countries in Europe and Asia also live in this city. Each group of people adds some of its traditions to Nairobi.

Nairobi is the largest and most modern city in Kenya. It is a city where many lawyers, doctors, and teachers work. Nairobi has tall apartment buildings and modern hospitals.

Not all of Kenya is like Nairobi. Smaller communities still follow traditional ways. Many people wear traditional clothing made of loose-fitting material that is wrapped around the body. In the villages of Kenya, there are no electric lights or running water. The roads are unpaved. Some village communities do not have schools.

Many people leave the villages to live in Nairobi. They look for work and hope life will be better there. Because so many villagers are moving to Nairobi, it is a very fast-growing city.

(above) Medical students in a hospital laboratory, Kenya   (right) Making monkey traps in a village in Kenya

Tourists from around the world visit Nairobi. Some take special trips into the countryside. These trips are called **safaris.** Kenya is famous for its animal wildlife. Elephants, lions, zebras, and giraffes are just a few of the animals people see on safaris. A safari is one way to learn about what is special in Kenya. Once people went on safaris to hunt animals. Today most safaris are for looking at animals or taking photographs.

This book has been a kind of safari, too. In it, you have learned about many communities. You have found answers to many questions. You have also discovered more questions to ask. Most of all, you have shared what is special about many different communities.

safari
a special trip taken into the African countryside to learn about wildlife

On a safari in Kenya

Section Review

Write your answers on a sheet of paper.
1. How did Nairobi get its name?
2. What is a safari?
3. Why do you think people from small villages in Kenya move to Nairobi?

241

African Cloth Coloring

Many parts of Africa are famous for the brilliant colors and bold patterns used in clothing. In Africa, the craft of coloring fabric goes back hundreds of years.

In the United States, coloring for cloth, or dye, can be bought in stores. But in Africa, the old ways of making dye are still used. Herbs and other plants are boiled in water. To make yellow dye, dandelions or marigolds are boiled. Onion skins or walnut shells can be boiled to make brown dye. Cloth is then dipped into the hot, colored liquid.

Nigeria and Cameroon are countries along the west coast of Africa. People in these countries are known for the special way they color fabric. American people call this method of coloring fabric "tie-dyeing."

The first step in tie-dyeing is to fold the cloth around a stick or stone. Twine is then tied tightly around the cloth. Next the material is painted with either one color of dye or with

a rainbow of colors. The dye does not touch the places where the cloth is folded or tied.

After the cloth is dry, it is untied and unfolded. If the cloth was tied around a large stone, a design that looks like a brightly colored sun appears. If the cloth was tied around a stick, a striped pattern is made.

In the United States today, you can buy clothes, sheets, and curtains with tie-dyed patterns. Some are dyed by hand and are very expensive. Others are done by machine. But there is another way to get tie-dyed fabric—do it yourself!

Instead of boiling herbs, you can buy ready-made dye. Rubber bands work as well as twine. The results are much like those in Nigeria or Cameroon—beautiful designs. No two patterns will ever be the same!

UNIT REVIEW

Word Work

Write the sentences below on a sheet of paper. Fill in the blanks with the correct words from the list.

monarchy　　current　　globe　　kibbutz

1. A model of the earth is called a ____.
2. The Hebrew word for "group" is ____.
3. The steady flow of water in one direction is called a ____.
4. A government headed by a king or queen is called a ____.

Knowing the Facts

Write your answers on a sheet of paper.

1. What group makes the laws of Great Britain?
2. Name two traditions people in Seto follow.
3. Why is Nairobi important to other nations in Africa?
4. Who makes decisions on a kibbutz?

Using What You Know

Choose one of the following activities to do. Follow the instructions given here.

1. Make a list of five places of interest to visit in London.
2. Pretend you have a friend in Seto, Hanita, or Nairobi. Write a letter to your friend that tells how your community is like or different from the community of Seto, Hanita, or Nairobi.

Skills Practice

Use the following maps to answer the questions below. Write your answers on a sheet of paper.

1. What imaginary line runs east to west around the globes in these pictures?
2. Which continents are in the Northern Hemisphere? Which continents are in both the Northern and Southern hemispheres?
3. How many continents are in only the Southern Hemisphere? What are their names?

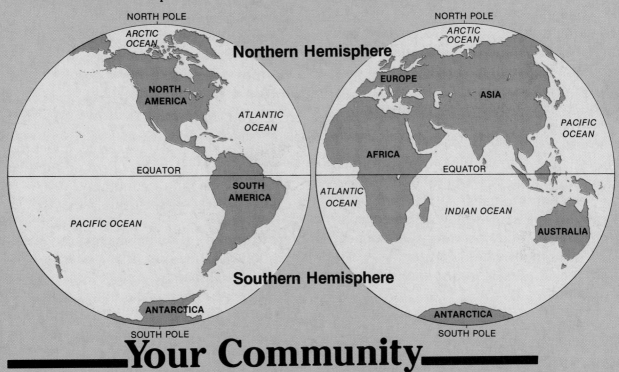

Your Community

People have come to the United States from many countries. They bring their country's traditions with them. Pretend you are going on a trip to London, Seto, Hanita, or Nairobi. What traditions from the United States would you take with you?

GLOSSARY

adobe brick made of mud and chopped straw

agriculture the business of farming

air pollution unclean, unsafe air

appoint to choose

arroyo a ditch formed by flood water

axis an imaginary straight line going through the earth from the North Pole to the South Pole

bar graph a picture using bars of different lengths to show information

bay a body of water partly surrounded by land

bayou a stream of slow-moving water that flows into or out of another body of water such as a river or bay

bituminous coal soft coal

boulevard a wide street often lined with trees

boundary the edge of a particular place, such as a town, city, or playground

cannery a factory where food products are put into cans

canyon a narrow valley with steep sides

channel a body of water that connects two other bodies of water

citizen a person who is a member of a community

citrus trees that bear certain kinds of fruit, such as lemons, limes, oranges, and grapefruit

city a large center where many people live and work

climate what the weather of an area is usually like over a long period of time

colony a place settled by people from another country and still ruled by that country

community a place and the people who live there

compass rose a drawing on a map that shows the direction of north, south, east, and west

conservation the preservation and protection of natural resources

consumer a person who buys and uses goods or services

continent one of the seven large bodies of land on the earth's surface

coquina a kind of stone made of the broken shells of many small sea animals

culture the way of life of a group of people who share a past, customs, beliefs, art, and often language

current the steady flow of water in one direction

custom the special way a group of people does something

dam a wall that controls the flow of water in a river

distance scale a measuring line on a map that can be used to tell how far one place is from another

district an area set aside for a special purpose

earthquake sudden shaking or trembling of the earth

elect to choose by voting

energy power to make things work

equator an imaginary line that runs east and west around the middle of the earth

erupt to explode

exchange a place where people give and receive information or help

factory a building where goods are manufactured

federal government the government of all the states together

flow chart a chart that uses arrows to show the order in which things happen

food processing making crops into food products

fork a place where rivers meet

globe a round model of the earth

goods things people make, such as shoes or chairs

government the group of people who manage a community, and their way of managing

growing season the period of time when crops are growing

gulf a large body of water with land almost all the way around it

harbor sheltered place where ships land

hemisphere half of the earth

hill a landform with sides that slope

human resources people whose work and skill are used by a community

humid damp

hurricane a storm with rain and very strong winds

immigrant a person who comes from another country to live in a new land

income money a person earns

industry producing things in factories or businesses

interstate highway a main road that connects communities in neighboring states

island a body of land entirely surrounded by water

kachina a Hopi Indian spirit

kibbutz a community in Israel in which all the people live and work as a group

lake a body of water surrounded by land

landform the shape of an area of land

landforms map a map that uses color to show the height and form of the land

landforms map a map that uses color to show the height and form of the land

landmark a building, statue, or place that is important or interesting

lava melted rock

laws rules that a government makes for the people in a community

leader a person who makes plans and helps show a community the best way to carry out these plans

limestone rock that was formed millions of years ago from the shells of some sea animals and the tiny skeletons, called coral, of others

manufacturing making a large number of products by machine

map a picture of a place

map key the part of a map that tells what the symbols mean

mayor head of a community government

memorial something built or done to help remember a person or event

mesa land with steep sides and a flat top

metropolitan area a city and the communities around it

mill a building with machines to make such things as flour or cloth

mineral a substance found in nature that is not an animal or a plant

mining the process of taking mineral resources from the earth

mission a community set up by a religious group

monarchy a government headed by a king or queen

monument something built to honor a person or event

mountain a tall landform with steep slopes

natural resources things we use from nature, such as water, air, soil, plants, and animals

ocean a large body of salt water that covers much of the earth's surface

Parliament a group of people who make the laws of Great Britain

peninsula land almost entirely surrounded by water

picture graph a chart that uses symbols to stand for information

pilgrim a person who makes a trip, often for religious reasons

pioneer a person who is the first to settle in a place

plain flat land

plantation a large farm where one crop is grown

plateau a high, flat stretch of land that is much larger than a mesa

plaza an open square in a town or city

prairie flat or rolling land that was once covered with tall grass

prime minister leader of Parliament and head of the British government

producer a person who makes goods or performs services

pueblo an Indian house built of mud and stone

quarry a place where stone is cut or blasted out of the ground

reclaim to make useful again

represent to speak or act for a person or group of people

responsibility duty

restore to rebuild buildings to look the way they did long ago

retire to stop working at a job after reaching a certain age

road map a guide to roads and highways, showing the ways to go from one place to another

rotate to turn or spin

safari a special trip taken into the African countryside to learn about wildlife

senior citizen an older person who has stopped working at a job

services useful acts that people do for others, often for money

settler a person who comes to make a home in a place

state capital the city where rules for the state are made

street map a map showing the streets of a neighborhood, town, or city

suburbs smaller communities that surround a city

surveyor a person who carefully measures land

symbol a small drawing that stands for something real

tax money that people must give to a government to pay for community needs

time line a graph that shows periods of time

timetable a chart that tells when buses, trains, or lanes arrive or leave

tourism the business of supplying services to visitors

tourist a visitor who comes to see the sights in a community

town a community that is smaller than a city

trader a person who buys and sells goods

tradition a custom followed over a long period of time

transportation ways of moving things from place to place

tribe a group of people with the same relatives, language, and customs

valley a low place between hills or mountains

volcano a mountain with an opening through which gas and rock can escape

volunteer a person who works without pay

water pollution dirtying of water by chemicals and waste materials

wilderness unsettled land

INDEX

(continued on next page)

ART CREDITS

PHOTO CREDITS